D0287798

A Flock of Eagles

a profile of the successful
life insurance agents and their association,
the Million Dollar Round Table

by Quaife M. Ward and Tedd C. Determan

Copyright © 1977 by the Million Dollar Round Table.
All Rights Reserved. Printed in the United States of
America. This book, or parts thereof, may not be reproduced in any form without permission of the publishers.

Book designed by Norm Ulrich and Clarke Krueger

In honor of
MARSHALL I. WOLPER, CLU
The Equitable Life Assurance Society of the United States
presents this book on the occasion of
the 50th Anniversary of the
Million Dollar Round Table.

TABLE OF CONTENTS

Page

Preface v

Introduction vii

1. WHERE EAGLES SOAR 1
   the life of the successful agent today

2. THE LAST OF THE GREAT ENTREPRENEURS 9
   the role of the agent in an institutionalized society

3. THE FLEDGLINGS 21
   how agents got started as individual entrepreneurs

4. TESTING THEIR WINGS 31
   the early road to professionalism

5. A FLOCK OF EAGLES................................ 41
   the first meeting of the Million Dollar Round Table

6. CATCHING THE UPDRAFTS 51
   the growth of the Round Table

7. THE MOST SUCCESSFUL SALESMEN IN THE WORLD 61
   a profile of the top producers

8. A GATHERING OF EAGLES 73
   the Annual Meeting

9. SELF-IMAGE...................................... 87
   how successful agents see themselves

10. BUILD A BETTER NEST 97
    the educational activities of the Round Table

11. THERE'S MORE TO LIFE THAN SELLING
    LIFE INSURANCE 105
    an explanation of the Whole Man Concept

12. SOARING INTO THE FUTURE 113
    an optimistic view of the future of the agent

Appendix:
A. ACKNOWLEDGEMENTS 118
B. ABOUT THE AUTHORS 119
C. BIBLIOGRAPHY 119
D. HISTORY OF MILLION DOLLAR ROUND TABLE 120
   a brief recounting of each year's activities

PREFACE

Eagles don't flock.

Eagles are individualists who mark off territories of their own choosing, then protect them. Eagles never flock together—yet if they did, there would be a gathering of some of the most majestic birds in the world.

There is a group of people who in some ways resemble the eagle in the lives they lead. They are the successful life insurance agents—members of the Million Dollar Round Table—and, like eagles, they soar with complete freedom to the highest pinnacles of achievement.

When these high-flying eagles gather together, they become that rarity . . . a flock of eagles . . . majestic human beings . . . the most successful group of sales personnel in the world . . . individualists brought together through a common bond . . . pioneers . . . the last of the great entrepreneurs.

The Million Dollar Round Table is the gathering place of these eagles, and to get there each agent must soar to spectacular heights. Yet theirs is perhaps the most misunderstood profession in the world. Few people understand—or appreciate—the career of the professional life underwriter.

This book has been published by the Million Dollar Round Table in commemoration of its 50th year of service to its members and to the public. It is the hope of the Executive Committee and the members of the Round Table that through this publication the real truth will be told about a career in the selling of life insurance—its excitements, its satisfactions, its great human service, its freedom, and its economic rewards.

It's a career to stimulate the minds of many.

It's not an easy career. Nor can a person arrive at the top without paying a price. But to those individualists, those pioneers, those rare entrepreneurs who are willing to take the risks and pay the price, this career offers the opportunity to sprout wings and soar to the highest levels of business and personal rewards—and eventually to join the only flock of eagles in the world.

Respectfully,
THE MILLION DOLLAR ROUND TABLE
1977 Executive Committee

Marshall I. Wolper, CLU, *President*
Rulon E. Rasmussen, CLU, *Immediate Past President*
Jack L. McKewen, CLU, *First Vice President*
Paul L. Oliver, Jr., CLU, *Second Vice President*
Millard J. Grauer, CLU, *Secretary*

INTRODUCTION

The greatest hazard to life is death. Untimely death—by accident, cancer, heart attack—can destroy an otherwise sound financial plan.

If a person knew for sure that he would live to be 70 years old, then he could plan a savings program that would guarantee his children's education and a comfortable retirement for himself and his spouse. But lifespans are not absolutely predictable, and that unpredictability has created the need for life insurance—one of the most remarkable and flexible financial instruments in the world.

It wasn't many years ago that when a spouse died, the surviving spouse and children were cared for by members of a supporting group. Sometimes the supporting group was the immediate family; or, in earlier times, support may have come from a guild or a feudal lord who provided for his chattel or from a clan or tribe in a close-knit village structure.

But modern life, and especially the free enterprise system, has created a situation in which each breadwinner has to make his own arrangements for his family's financial security in the event that he dies.

In response to this situation, the life insurance industry was born. Life insurance gave each breadwinner the chance to belong to a group, thereby pooling his risk with that of others so that the family of each was protected in the event of untimely death. A life insurance company, by the sale of a life insurance policy, would assume the risk of a breadwinner dying.

Life insurance benefits not only individuals but also society as a whole. Over the years life insurance companies have built large reserves based on the money that policyholders have paid in premiums. These reserves have helped to stimulate the economy. One company builds a new plant . . . another buys machinery and equipment . . . another builds a housing project

. . . another buys airplanes for its fleet . . . all from life insurance company loans of reserve funds.

The amount of life insurance in force, which produced these reserves, is so staggering that it defies the imagination. The face value of policies in force is in the trillions of dollars.

The reserves, which support this fantastic figure, are invested back into the economy and have given the life insurance industry rock-like stability. During the Depression of the 1930s, when other financial institutions floundered, the life insurance companies, on the strength of their assets, rode out the storm relatively unscathed.

How was such a tremendous pool of capital created? Who was responsible?

Enter the life insurance agent, who sells the insurance policies . . .

. . . that create the payments . . .

. . . that build the reserves . . .

. . . that are reinvested and help the economy grow . . .

. . . and that guarantee to pay a certain sum in the future in the event of:

       retirement (living benefits)
       unforeseen permanent disability
       or untimely death

No other financial tool in the history of the world has offered the advantages that life insurance offers to those who buy it, to the economy at large, and to those who sell it.

Yet life insurance is a difficult product to sell for a number of reasons.

It's an intangible.

It competes for the same dollars that could be used for a person's recreation and enjoyment.

And it forces a person to think about a rather unpleasant aspect of life . . . death!

The successful life insurance agent must rattle the brain of his client with future shock. He must grip his client's intellect and shout:

"You insure your house although you're not certain it's going to burn down!

"You insure your car although you're not certain you'll have an accident!

"So why in blazes won't you insure your most valuable asset, the only asset you cannot replace, your own life, when you know with absolute certainty that you're going to die?"

This is the story of these unusual men and women . . . of the system of selling that spawned them . . . of their development into professionals . . . of the Million Dollar Round Table, the dynamic organization they have built . . .

. . . and of why, like eagles, these extraordinary people have soared higher and farther than others.

CHAPTER ONE

Where Eagles Soar

Nothing is impossible!
Anything is possible!
Diversity . . . the key to life!
No two days are alike!
A world of freedom!
A spectrum of life!
Involvement!

Enter the world of the successful life insurance agent:

- a world of freedom, where an agent can be what he wants to be, do what he wants to do;
- a world of great financial rewards;
- a world of diversity, where no two days are alike;
- a world of excitement, travel, and honors;
- a world of honest friendships and the giving and sharing that go with them;
- a world of intensely-held beliefs;
- a world of tender joys and deeply felt sorrows;
- a world that challenges the mind and commits the heart.

The successful life insurance agent's world includes such a wide spectrum of action-packed activities and such a variety of ego-satisfying fulfillments that few ever retire in the traditional sense.

Most of the producers started with next to nothing, so they're proud of their incomes. Many earn hundreds of thousands of dollars a year, more than the presidents of the world's largest corporations. They drive prestige cars, live in waterfront homes, fly their own airplanes, send their children to the finest colleges and universities, and travel the world first-class.

Yet money as a goal is seldom on the top of any producer's list. The money is there, and they earn every cent of it. They're proud of it, and they enjoy it. But it's not their primary goal.

More important than money itself is the freedom success brings. Unlike the corporate executive, to whom success often brings an isolated confinement to an ivory tower, the successful life insurance agent is like a high-soaring eagle—free to pursue a dream, target on a goal, and live his life according to the dictates of his own conscience and his own wants and needs.

Take these examples:

- One agent and his wife are sailing their boat around the world;
- Another started the nationwide Medic-Alert program (where a person with an illness such as diabetes wears a tag identifying the affliction) that has saved hundreds of lives;
- Another is the governor of his state, while many others are ambassadors, congressmen, mayors;
- One, who was born to a poor, sharecropping family, is a trustee of a prestigious university in his state;
- Many others appear as prized lecturers at leading universities and before other professionals such as accountants, lawyers, and bankers;
- Many are financial advisors far afield from the life insur-

ance business, serving on the boards of some of the largest corporations in the world;

- A large number have achieved such greatness that they are listed in Who's Who in America, Who's Who in the World, and Who's Who in Finance and Industry.

The dreams, goals, and lifestyles of successful producers are as diverse as the people themselves. The key is that when they reach the top they have a freedom of movement seldom found in any other profession.

One day is never the same as the next in the diverse world of these top producers. In their profession they deal with such a wide variety of clients with so many needs that a top producer's daily "action list" reads like an encyclopedia of human involvement.

Here's a sampling of the calls made by one successful agent in a single day:

- Met with two attorneys, two accountants, and a consulting actuary to resolve tax problems on a client's pension/profit sharing plan;
- Set up a group insurance plan for a young Moroccan woman starting a new retail business;
- Wrote a mortgage policy for a young couple buying their first home;
- Worked out a life insurance funded stock redemption agreement among shareholders in a chain store business;
- Consulted with a manufacturer's representative on tax shelters;
- Helped a client rearrange his estate in preparation for his forthcoming divorce;
- Consulted with a client and friend who had been given only a few days to live because of cancer; rearranged the estate to provide money for the wife and children, thereby saving them over $25,000 in taxes;

- Set up a quarterly meeting with the widow of a friend and her advisors, consulting on both financial and personal matters (her son wants to start a rock band);
- Wrote a policy covering the college education of a newborn child;
- Called a client to remind him that he forgot to take a physical examination;
- Informed a client that his premium would be substantially increased because of his ulcerated colitis condition; tried, without luck, to place the insurance with another company for a smaller premium;
- In competition with other agents, submitted a proposal for a split-funded pension plan.

This list represents just part of one agent's activities for one day. But even in this sampling the range of contacts and the diversity of emotions are incredible, from the excitement of helping to set up a new business to the emotional trauma of working with a man going through a divorce; from the joy of assisting a young couple in buying their first home to the sadness of talking with a dying friend, coupled with the professional pride of being able to save the survivors' money; from the serene pleasure of writing a policy to guarantee the college education of a newborn child to the challenge of competing with someone else to secure new business.

Yet this was not an unusual day for this agent. Because of his chosen profession, each day is as diverse as the previous one—each requiring him to draw on his sophisticated knowledge of the life insurance business, plus demanding an emotional involvement that comes from knowing, understanding, and being a part of the personal lives and financial concerns of his clients.

And even this amazing range of activities does not represent the complete world of the successful life insurance agent. Here are some of the activities pursued during a year in the life of one of the near-legendary producers in the Round Table.

Consider that the man started selling life insurance just over 20 years before, in a city where he was a total stranger, with only $300 to his name. His annual income now exceeds six figures per year. In the course of one year this man:

- Spoke at a conference of life insurance agents in Malaga, Spain; took his sons on a tour of Spain, Portugal, and Morocco;
- Attended shows in Las Vegas on the way to a Round Table committee meeting in Arizona;
- Placed a multi-million-dollar policy on the life of a builder to protect his associates should he die before completing a 1,000-apartment complex;
- Testified in Washington, D.C., before a congressional committee on a new tax reform act;
- Convinced an Internal Revenue Service agent not to assess additional tax on a client in the children's wear manufacturing business;
- Lectured at the graduate business school of a state university on the applications of life insurance in the business world;
- Worked with a computer programmer to update an office computer to enable it to handle the provisions of the new pension reform act;
- Made a triangle trip to California, Hawaii, and Alaska, selling major policies to a group of heart surgeons in California, a resort complex in Hawaii, and an electronics firm in Alaska;
- Took a polar flight from Alaska to London to speak before a convention of life insurance agents in the United Kingdom and received the honor of being escorted in by the Royal Coldstream Guard;
- Consulted with the widow of a client and friend whose two daughters were completing college at Harvard and Yale, all of whom were enjoying a lifestyle that would

have been out of the question except for their life insurance benefits;

- Made several speeches before a local bar association and CPA group on the provisions of the new pension reform act;
- Went on a speaking tour of all six states of Australia and was treated like royalty; also went scuba diving off the Great Barrier Reef and along the beautiful reefs of Tahiti on the way back;
- In New York, met with the president of one of the world's largest pharmaceutical firms to discuss a life insurance based compensation program for his top executives;
- Delivered a check for $800,000 to the widow of a young doctor who died in an airplane crash on his way back from a hunting trip—money that meant the difference between near poverty and a continued affluent lifestyle for the widow and her children;
- Worked on the successful campaign of a client running for mayor;
- Met with a managing partner of one of the nation's largest accounting firms regarding a death benefit program for his junior partners;
- Made a joint proposal with a Connecticut agent for a pension plan for a large law firm;
- Attended by invitation a "think-tank" session of the nation's business leaders at Brookings Institute;
- Conducted an in-depth seminar on pensions for the members of the Round Table.

These are but a handful of the highlights from one year in the life of one successful agent. Between these highlights the agent engages in typical days like the one outlined earlier. Although the details differ from agent to agent, this is nonetheless a realistic example of the dynamic, mind-expanding, and exciting world of involvement that is the domain of the highest flying eagles in the insurance business.

The single factor that holds this whirlwind of activity together, that gives it all meaning, is the successful underwriter's intensely held belief that life insurance is the greatest financial tool in the history of the world for guaranteeing future financial security.

No matter how many honors an agent receives, this belief is reinforced nearly every day. For example, another agent received the most prestigious award in the life insurance industry, with a huge banquet in his honor. The very next day he personally delivered a death claim check to the nearly impoverished family of a man he had insured many years before. For the surviving family that check made the difference between welfare lines and a comfortable life, between the degradation of government handouts and the dignity and freedom that comes from being financially secure.

That's the spectrum of life in the world of the successful life insurance agent . . .

. . . a life full of challenges and rewards . . .
. . . a life of constant diversity . . .
. . . a life of joys and sorrows . . .
. . . a life of freedom to pursue dreams . . .
. . . a life of friendships and commitments . . .
. . . a life of deeply held beliefs.

It's a rewarding life. For the right person, it's the most exciting career on earth.

CHAPTER TWO

The Last of the Great Entrepreneurs

There is a basic contradiction in the world of every life insurance agent. On the one hand he's selling a product that minimizes the risk of financial loss because of untimely death or disability. He dedicates his life to convincing prospects of this risk and the need for life insurance to cover it.

On the other hand the agent himself leads a life of risk by being in a business where failure is common. The risk involves more than just starting a new business and being self-employed, even though that risk is considerable given the high percentage of small business failures worldwide.

The risk to a life insurance agent is heightened by the fact that he's selling an intangible product that requires a level of selling sophistication that can come only through education, training, and experience—but mainly experience. So, right from the beginning, he knows that the start-up period required until he achieves a level of sophistication could involve considerable sacrifice. Compounding this risk is the fact that most starting agents do not have a cushion of family wealth or other sources of income that could tide them over the "dry," or "slump," periods that even the old-timers in the business encounter.

Developing a convincing approach may not dispel the risk. An agent may take months or years to cultivate prospects, only to find that they are not insurable. A medical exam may turn up heart disease or cancer that the prospect was unaware of.

More risks to the life insurance agent come through a changing marketplace. New tax laws can suddenly make an agent's selling situation much less attractive, after he has spent years educating himself and developing techniques to sell clients on the basis of the tax situation. Mass merchandising of life insurance directly to the consumer can cut into the markets that an agent has spent years nurturing.

Nor are all the risks economic. The starting agent may be assailed by negative stereotypes of the profession that tend to stigmatize the agent and especially give doubts to the younger agent about his choice of profession.

In a very real sense, the successful life insurance underwriter is the last of the great entrepreneurs. He has challenged all these risks; he has pitted his own ability against seemingly insurmountable odds; and he has conquered them all!

The odds against a beginning agent's survival are great. Seventy-five percent of the agents hired today won't be in the business three years from now. But once an agent has been in the business four years, the chances are nine out of ten that he'll remain in it for life.

Although many life insurance companies have made tremendous efforts to decrease the turnover rate, it's still difficult to predict whether a young agent will succeed in the profession. It takes a rare combination of qualities to make a successful agent—one of the last of the great entrepreneurs.

Nations of the free world were built on the efforts of the individual entrepreneur, the person who was willing to put himself on the line—to risk all—in order to pursue his personal dream of success. These were not the Carnegies, the Rhodes, the Vanderbilts, or the Rockefellers—who are showcase examples—but the average guy who was willing to test himself and his ideas in wide-open countries that were receptive to individual initiative.

The risk of starting a farm in Minnesota or of running a barge down the Mississippi, of starting a mining operation in Australia or a citrus grove in Israel, was seldom thought of as a risk but rather as a challenge. The early entrepreneurs knew that if they worked hard no one would prevent them from succeeding. This was in sharp contrast to the life most of the immigrants had known. In their native countries, which often had caste systems, hard work meant simply more hard work, with little opportunity to profit from labor or new ideas.

Work hard! Succeed! The sky's the limit! These were the enticements of the "new" lands of the United States, Canada, and Australia. And men and women flocked to these and other lands where they would have the chance to pursue their personal dreams.

Anyone who has traveled throughout the free world has seen the enormous production capability that is evident in virtually every city, town, and farming area—all a tribute to the hundreds of thousands of individual entrepreneurs, the men and women who had dreams and pursued them. No one will read about most of these men and women in history books. But history has recorded the cumulative effect of their individual initiative, which resulted in the greatest free enterprise systems the world has ever known.

Top life insurance agents are among the last of the great entrepreneurs because, contrary to modern attitudes, they remain willing to target on a dream and follow it no matter what the sacrifice. Their beliefs may be nearly obsolete, but their successes speak for themselves.

Despite the fact that most free societies owe their very being to the free exercise of individual initiative, these same societies are today instituting policies that squelch individual initiative.

Governments employ larger and larger work forces, either directly or indirectly. Multinational businesses demand conformity. Big unions homogenize the once individualistic flair of artisans. These all-encompassing institutions smother the individual with numbered anonymity and numbing mediocrity and have combined to produce a society where individual initiative is second to conformity.

Cradle-to-the-grave security is the order of the day. A person is born a number, dies a number, and wonders in between who he is! This situation has encouraged those who feel that the world owes them a living. "I ask not what I can give, but what I can receive," seems to be the prevailing attitude. There is more and more reliance on government welfare programs such as unemployment compensation and a ballooning social security system.

Today's system is destructive to individual initiative and responsibility. A college graduate who considers himself independent, creative, and "tuned in to his inner self" will nevertheless spend hours standing in line for a government welfare or unemployment check while jobs he considers unworthy of his talents go begging.

In earlier days individuals solved problems by working them out with other individuals. Today the tendency is to lean on institutions. A person cries "whiplash" the minute his car is nudged; the uninjured pedestrian who stumbles on the sidewalk or curb seeks damages; the slightest surgical or medical discrepancy is regarded as grounds for a malpractice suit. The assumption is that everyone is insured against "risk" and that marginal and nuisance claims will be paid. It comes as no surprise that this "Sue! . . . Sue! . . . Sue!" philosophy has produced jammed courtrooms.

Certainly individual initiative exists today within the confines of big businesses or governmental institutions, where many creative minds are being put to use. But the initiative is still stifled under the umbrella of security that reflects the wants and needs of so many workers. The regular paycheck with all the benefits named earlier is so much a part of the expectations that to be denied this umbrella of security is, for many, a major catastrophe.

In spite of these trends there is a small, special corps of individualists—people who are willing to do what so few in today's societies are willing even to consider. These special people whole-heartedly adopt the creed that whatever they achieve shall be based upon their own efforts, their own abilities, and their own stick-to-itiveness—and that they'll take the headaches as well as the rewards!

These beliefs are what make the top life insurance agents such a back-to-the-roots type of group.

They're dissimilar in appearance.

They have different backgrounds.

They talk differently.

They relate to their clients using a wide variety of techniques.

But these men and women have one thing in common. They share that founding-father, back-to-the-Constitution, open-the-West, on-to-the-gold fields set of ideals and beliefs that typified the early entrepreneur.

Few occupations demand the individual resourcefulness required of the successful life insurance agent. And few offer such handsome financial rewards coupled with deep personal satisfaction.

That the leading producers were able to use their ingenuity to profit from such a risky business places them, as a group, among the last of the great entrepreneurs.

They faced the unknown.

They worked hard.

They dedicated themselves to excellence.

And they won.

The top underwriters exude self-confidence, and they have a

right to. Everything they have they've earned by their own efforts. Although many of them express surprise that they have succeeded to such a degree, they nonetheless are openly proud of their achievements. And, what's more, they enjoy their hard-earned wealth.

Yet even when they get to the top, these men and women reveal a remarkable dichotomy. They have spent their careers dealing heavily in matters of finance, yet they possess a surprising degree of sensitivity and concern for people.

They're hard-nosed but soft-hearted.

One great Past President of the Round Table will become downright impatient with prospects who won't insure "the necessities and common decencies of life for loved ones." Yet he will reach into his own pocket to pay the premiums of a policyholder with financial difficulties.

Another veteran member will spend hours and sometimes days disciplining himself for a big sale, toughening his mind so that he can communicate clearly with a prospect. Yet in the drawer of his desk are the policies of all his deceased policyholders. He will often weep when he opens that drawer.

Sometimes this agent uses his emotional commitment to his profession as a weapon. Heaven help the poor prospect who says something disparaging about life insurance! At the first sign of such an attitude, the agent will open the center drawer and carefully place each of the policies, one by one, in the prospect's hands while recounting the tragedy that each policy represents and telling how life insurance saved the survivors from disaster. It's an emotional scene that takes a lot out of him, but it carries a basic impact about the importance of life insurance that the prospect will never forget.

"If you don't feel it and don't believe in this business," this veteran tells younger agents, "then get out of it, and don't clutter up the field!"

Although most of the top underwriters don't carry their emotional commitment so close to the surface, they all have it and feel very deeply about their own deceased clients. A good part of this is because, on their way to the top, they become good friends with many of their clients. Chances are that when a client dies, the agent is also losing a close friend. So the dead client list of any agent is supercharged with emotion.

One of the most sophisticated members of the Round Table was a past president from Chicago. He was a debonair, dashing man, who in his later years traveled among the social elite of the city. Yet every morning he would sit down with a list of his clients who had died and think about what he had done for the survivors. He was recharging his missionary zeal.

Because of this commitment agents seldom completely retire from the business. Unlike business and industry executives, who are forced to retire, the Million Dollar Round Table member can continue to work at his own pace, for as long as he wishes. Most have worked out modified retirement plans that allow them to continue producing while at the same time pursuing sometimes elaborate personal dreams.

Another past president of the Round Table recently sold the largest policy of his career at age 77. His first-year commission on that policy alone will exceed $100,000. A week after the sale he left for a two-month vacation. An avid horseman, he was off to the hunts in South Carolina.

Round Table members apply the same advanced estate planning concepts to their own lives as they do with clients. They start with a dream and plan their estates accordingly.

A successful 42-year-old producer in the eastern United States has a dream of owning a home in Bermuda with a yacht capable of taking him to Europe and the Mediterranean. Through a carefully prepared plan, based mainly upon placing his renewal commissions into an investment program and living on his first-year commissions, he plans to accomplish his dream at the age of 53—the same year his youngest child will enter college. He also plans to keep an apartment in his home city and continue working for perhaps six months of each year. Will he realize his dream?

Many do!

One member entered the business at age 31 with the dream of sailing around the world at age 51. Now in his mid-50s, he and his wife are sailing their 45-foot yawl on the dream voyage he had planned. They return to the mainland for a few weeks each year, and during that time he sells enough new business to qualify him as one of the top producers in the Round Table.

Stories abound within the Round Table about members who pursued their personal dreams and made them happen.

One became an ambassador.

One became the governor of his state.

Many became missionaries for their churches.

One became a recognized mountain climber.

The realization of a dream requires more than desire. One legendary producer thought he had a perfect plan for his first years in the profession. He reasoned that his wife's earnings would carry them through his rough start-up period. Within three months his wife suffered a serious injury in a fall, thus cutting off her earnings. He had to work even harder. Despite the sacrifices, he credits much of his later success to the discipline he had to develop during those early years.

Nearly every top producer has his own story of the problems he had to solve and the sacrifices he had to make in his early days. Many of the most successful agents had doubts about their careers even after they'd been in the business for years, especially during dry spells, or slumps, when they couldn't seem to sell anyone anything.

One large-volume producer once got so discouraged that he answered a blind advertisement in his local newspaper for a job that offered "unlimited potential for the right man." As it turned out, the ad had been placed by his own general agent.

Yet despite, or sometimes because of, the doubts and early

start-up problems the top producers develop a mental toughness and optimism that carry them through the down periods.

Over the years the top producers develop another trait that is common to all of them—the ability to express an idea simply, without using five-dollar words. Even speaking extemporaneously, these agents use a minimum of words to get an idea across. Most of them went through periods when they tried to overwhelm their clients with their knowledge—until they learned that they weren't communicating their messages. Once at the top, even when dealing with the most complex estate plans, these agents strive for a mature simplicity in their presentations to clients.

They develop what they call "power phrases," which are catchy combinations of words expressing ideas that strike the interest or imagination of the client. Many top producers are masters of the power phrase. Even in a casual conversation the stimulating one-liners pour out of them:

"I have never found a good substitute for money."

"You can't solve a permanent problem with temporary insurance."

"May I show you how much of what you own isn't yours?"

At their best, these phrases are delivered with the timing of a top comedian. However, they're used not for a laugh, but to punctuate a thought or to drive home a crucial point.

Although these may sound like "tricks of the trade," they underline the fervent desire of the underwriter to communicate most effectively those concepts which the average client finds difficult to grasp. They are but another example of the creativity and dedication that the top producers bring to their profession.

In the face of enormous odds against their very survival in the business . . .

Starting with nothing but unlimited optimism and belief in themselves . . .

Developing discipline and tough-mindedness . . .

Cultivating a basic interest in people into a messianic zeal for a product and its ability to help people . . .

Balancing hard-nosed money talk with compassion . . .

Striving to reduce the complex money needs of a person in a complex society to understandable simplicity . . .

Taking the many risks of the self-employed person who profits only from his own efforts . . .

. . . the top life insurance underwriter today survives as one of the last of the great entrepreneurs—a pioneer in a society in which individual pioneers have become almost obsolete.

Will this pioneering breed continue to enter the profession? Or will our age of the computer, our age of technocracy, devise ways to circumvent the agent and deal directly with the consumer? Will one of the few remaining bastions of free enterprise die in the government-controlled, big-business economy that is here today?

The top producers don't think so: they're not worried; they're not afraid. They face the future optimistically, knowing that the experience and talents that brought them success in the past will continue to do so in the future.

CHAPTER THREE

The Fledglings

The life insurance agent is unique in history.

He's a self-employed entrepreneur, yet he works for one of the world's largest industries.

He sells an intangible commodity with almost missionary zeal to a skeptical buyer who doesn't understand the product and who often looks with suspicion on the person selling it.

He draws on a sophisticated knowledge of estate and financial planning.

He resembles the popular stereotype of the life insurance agent about as much as an eagle resembles a toad.

Agents are individualists. Yet as individualistic as they are, they do share common traits—traits like hard work and belief in family and handshake honesty that all sound corny in today's world where wives and husbands are as disposable as diapers.

The successful life insurance agent has always been a self-starting entrepreneur. He has to be in order to survive, because his income has always been based on commissions. The more he sells, the more he makes.

In the early days the agents were peddlers, fledglings selling a new and sophisticated means of protection against the financial loss incurred when the breadwinner of a family dies. At first the policies were intended mainly to cover burial costs or to pay off a mortgage or a bank loan.

Over the years the agents and the product they sold became more sophisticated. Instead of offering life insurance only as a means of paying off immediate debts, the successful agents were able to convince clients to insure the continuity of their family's lifestyle, to insure the continuation of a business if a partner died, to provide additional income on retirement, or to preserve an estate against inheritance taxes.

Today the successful life insurance agent is a professional. The basic concept is still the same—offering protection against the financial loss caused by an untimely death—but the applications in a modern society are so varied that an agent must have a working knowledge of state and federal tax laws, banking regulations, business law, accounting principles, and medical procedures, not to mention the tremendous complexities of the insurance business and the many laws that govern it.

The story of how the life insurance agent developed from peddler to professional has no parallel in history. An unusual breed of person has evolved—a type of person who combines an entrepreneurial zest for making money with a missionary zeal for the important role his product plays in modern society.

Let's dip back in history a bit and see the factors that contributed to make life insurance agents what they are today.

The year was 1807. In Philadelphia the first life insurance agent in the United States, Israel Whelen, began selling for Pelican Life Insurance Company of London.

Whelen must have been a lonely optimist. Lonely, because it took months for a message to travel to his home office and back, even on the fastest sailing ships. Optimist, because who would buy a product that few people understood from a company located in a country that was still regarded by many as an enemy?

Whelen lasted three years before Pennsylvania outlawed foreign competition. There is no record of his sales or commissions. His was a tiny spark, extinguished quickly. Like too many who came later, Whelen was a part-timer; his primary job was the selling of fire insurance.

Twenty years later, in 1830, the New York Life Insurance and Trust Company (not the same as today's New York Life) appointed agents—mostly lawyers and bankers—throughout the state to make real estate loans. Later these representatives began underwriting life insurance as a sideline business.

These local agents received no advances or salary. When they sold a policy, they received a commission. Because they were bankers and lawyers, they generally had a wealthy clientele—businessmen and land owners who bought life insurance to secure loans and leases. If an agent was alert and understood the basics of life insurance, he was able to sell a small policy to pay for a client's burial expenses.

Other companies were offering life insurance at this time, but no one was out selling it. If a buyer wanted it, he had to go to the company office and sign up. New York Life, by appointing registered agents, simply increased the number of places a client could walk into, but the buyer still had to take the initiative.

Despite the fact that this seems like a passive way to sell life insurance, the New York Life agency system proved so successful that the company soon outdistanced its competitors.

New York Life's moderate success notwithstanding, the potential market for life insurance hadn't even begun to be tapped. By 1840, a full 10 years after New York Life set up its system, there were only 15 life companies with about $4,700,000 worth of policies in force.

In the 1840s the mutual life insurance companies started. "Life insurance at cost," they said, meaning the policyholders "mutually" owned the companies. And the United States was ready for them!

The Industrial Revolution was starting. Railroads, canals, and steamboats gave people greater mobility. The lands to the west were opening up. The changes brought by new inventions and the increased mobility opened the mind to new ideas, new ways of doing things—and life insurance jumped right in.

The mutuals represented a new idea. They sold life insurance exclusively. Although the companies had little capital, the founders were ambitious and hard-working, and they knew a little about life insurance theory. They saw the mutual concept offering them the power, position, and wealth they sought without having to come up with the capital required to form a stock company.

The founders of the new mutuals looked to the success of New York Life's agency setup and to the structure of the life companies then operating in London. They couldn't afford a staff of salaried agents, so they relied on a large number of commissioned agents to bring the product to the consumer as quickly as possible.

No one really understood at the time how to sell life insurance, including the founders of the mutuals. But they were astute and hungry enough to understand that the product had to get to the buyer. They chose to accomplish this through commissioned agents who actively went out and sold.

The mutuals were ambitious. They wanted their product in everyone's hands immediately, which meant having as many agents as possible selling in as many locations as possible. Since the home office couldn't readily interview prospective agents in every city, it assigned a territory to an established agent and gave him the responsibility of engaging and directing a sales force for that territory. Thus was born the general agency system.

In those early days life insurance was an unusual product that few prospective buyers understood. But the concept of affiliating with others to protect one's family in the event of untimely death was attractive to a practical-minded public with a tradition of accepting family responsibilities.

The theory of life insurance made a lot of sense. But transferring that theory into the reality of a sale was another matter. Because there was no training, the agent and general agent simply went out and learned by doing—using whatever literature was available from the home office and then getting to the consumer and directly promoting the sale.

The agents must have done a fairly convincing job. Sales of the mutuals soared. Seven of the mutuals organized between 1835 and 1947 have survived to the present day and rank among the top 25 life insurance companies in the world.

One of the major reasons for the mutuals' initial success was the low cost of selling the product. The company paid the agent nothing until the agent made a sale. Typically, the company was able to get an agent started with a cash outlay of next to nothing—a letter of appointment, a few booklets, rate sheets, application forms and, in rare cases, a small advertising allowance.

With such a minimal start-up cost, the companies reasoned, why not get as many agents as possible out selling the product? And so they did, hiring every warm body that came along. It didn't matter that one agent was willing to spend 70 to 80 hours a week while another might spend only four or five. The companies lost no money on the less ambitious agents, because each agent was paid only according to what he sold. So all agents were treated alike, and the companies gave them all an equal amount of training—none!

The United States was in a period of tremendous, surging growth. The California gold rush was on, and the spirit of rushing headlong into unknown territories for unheard of wealth was the same spirit of American business. The early mutuals were like gold mines, and other entrepreneurs rushed headlong into the race for the life insurance dollar.

In 1865 there were about 4,000 agents.

By 1916 there were over 150,000 agents.

In just 50 years the number of agents multiplied almost 40 times, indicating the immense growth of the life insurance industry.

Statistics tell the growth but not the penalties paid by such rapid growth. One of the worst was that the agent was still relatively untrained and uneducated. Anyone with a smile, bravura, and a glib tongue could talk his way into selling for some company. Too often, untrained and uneducated agents were out on the streets selling a product that had a great deal to do with another person's future financial security. But at the same time there existed a large core of career agents who did a creditable job of selling life insurance.

As the industry grew and became more prosperous, so did the agent. Although commissions varied from company to company, the average level was at least five times higher after the Civil War than when the mutual companies started the big push forward in 1840.

From the very beginning, however, the agent received little support from the company he worked for. Agents were regarded as outside the corporate family, despite the fact that they were the marketing arms of their companies. This attitude forced the agents to be self-starters, entrepreneurs in the real sense, in order to survive. So the individual initiative that still characterizes life insurance agents today got its start in the very beginning.

An exception to this hands-off attitude of the companies was Henry Baldwin Hyde, who started the Equitable Life Assurance Society of the United States in 1859, when he was 25 years old.

Hyde was one of the most remarkable individuals in the history of the life insurance business. Starting with little more than a name for his company, he had 200 agents in the field within two years. Ten years after he started, Equitable had surpassed all other insurance companies in annual sales.

Within 26 years the assets of Equitable made it the largest life insurance company in the world.

Hyde was one of the few early moguls to understand the need for a highly motivated sales force. He concentrated his efforts on his selling team, encouraging them and stimulating them with sales ideas like no one had done before. That his company became number one so quickly is a tribute to Hyde's recognition of the importance of agents.

In fact, the story is told that Hyde once left a meeting of the top bankers and business executives in New York City in order to talk with one of his best agents. "With our bank balances," he reportedly said, "we can get all the bankers we want. But a top agent is hard to find."

Few companies followed Hyde's lead, and as the century neared a close, agents were still treated as peddlers, still not receiving any training before they started to sell.

In the meantime the industry was suffering some severe growing pains. Throughout their history, life insurance companies have nearly always been models of integrity. But competition, and in some cases a touch of greed, brought about some severe abuses of the life insurance concept, which led to a major investigation of the industry in 1906.

Although students of the life insurance business regard this investigation as a major turning point in the industry, it really wasn't directed at the agents, who were generally regarded as pawns. Some practices that involved agents, such as rebating part of a commission to a client, were forbidden, but most of the regulatory legislation that followed the investigation was aimed at abuses such as insurance policies that didn't pay off as promised by the companies and money manipulation practices engaged in by some company officials.

Because the agents were the front-line representatives of the companies, the scandal rubbed off on them. But it's a tribute to the selling abilities of insurance agents that the life insurance business survived the national scandal.

First, despite their peddler image the agents had done a good job over the previous 65 years of convincing the public of the value of life insurance. Even though in 1906 consumers were disgusted by some company practices, they still endorsed the concept of life insurance and still believed in the local agents with whom they did business.

Also, the agents had sold so much life insurance over the years that the large companies were financially sound.

As the United States entered the 20th century, agents began to realize the need for an increasing professionalism. They had been fledglings long enough.

Now it was time to test their wings.

Tom Kowal

CHAPTER FOUR

Testing Their Wings

The life insurance agent's rise to professionalism didn't happen all of a sudden. It was, rather, a gradual maturing process that started near the end of the 19th century and gained considerable momentum following the 1906 investigation of the life insurance industry.

The fact that the industry not only survived but rose above these difficult periods is due in part to some of the agents themselves. In the midst of the competitive maelstrom that brought about so many of the abuses that caused the investigation, there remained a strong core of agents who believed in their product, fought for fair treatment of their customers, and tried to upgrade their occupation.

Agents began to test their wings as professionals as early as 1869, when they started to organize local associations to improve the then chaotic marketing conditions. In the 1870s such associations sprang up in Cincinnati, Pittsburgh, Boston, Maine, and several Southern states.

In 1890, representatives of the 14 existing local life underwriter associations met in Boston to form the National Association of Life Underwriters (NALU). Its purpose was to provide a national forum in which the agents could seek solutions to the many problems that were unique to them.

Agents wanted to eliminate practices, such as rebating, that unfairly tarnished the image of the vast majority of underwriters who didn't get involved in such unethical kickbacks. They knew that most of the life insurance companies weren't doing anything to improve the marketing conditions, so they sought to accomplish as a group what they couldn't do individually.

By the time the investigation hit in 1906, NALU members had convinced 20 states to establish anti-rebating laws. Because of these positive efforts NALU members were the only life insurance representatives invited to a Presidential conference held after the investigation to decide what measures should be taken to correct conditions in the life insurance business.

Although the start of the new century marked a low for the insurance business, it was also the start of a new period for the agent—a period of learning about the business, of gradually increasing sophistication in dealing with new applications for life insurance, and of new programs that would change the agent's image from that of a peddler to a respected professional.

Some of these changes came about because of altered economic conditions. For example, up to that time the life insurance agent had sold relatively small policies that paid for burial costs or that represented an investment that would pay handsome dividends in a person's old age.

But after 1906 changing conditions demanded more sophisticated selling. Increasing competition from several new sources began to squeeze full-time agents out of the small policy market.

In the face of this increasing competition the resourceful agents sought new, more lucrative markets. But to succeed in these markets, the agents needed a higher degree of training and education. The question then became: How could the agents get this expanded knowledge? Could they turn to the logical source, the companies that sold the product? No, because the agents were outsiders, independent entrepreneurs whose fortunes were made or lost by virtue of their own selling ability.

Instead, the agents turned to the one resource they had always depended on—themselves. They did what agents have been doing ever since: they educated themselves by pooling their knowledge.

One of the most successful producers at the turn of the century was Edward A. Woods, a general agent of the Equitable Society in Pittsburgh. Just as Henry Hyde exemplifies the founders of the life insurance business, Woods is a great example of the type of leadership the agents had at the start of the push for professionalism.

Woods was one of those rare people who, because they're so deeply committed to what they do, are always in the vanguard. Consider these examples of Woods' foresight:

His agency was one of the first to sell large quantities of group insurance.

Woods was among the first to understand the concept of the economic value of a human life, the need for assigning a monetary value to earning power; and he effectively used this concept as a sales tool.

Woods urged his agents to prospect in high-income markets and to sell large volumes of high-premium insurance.

He was one of the first to understand and market business insurance to both individual proprietors and partnerships.

He pioneered the concept of selling life insurance to provide a monthly retirement income rather than a lump sum settlement.

He was among the first—as early as 1911—to recognize the opportunities for using life insurance as a means to lessen the impact of inheritance taxes.

A partial measure of Woods' success is reflected in the amount of life insurance his agency had in force in the following years:

```
1890 — $  10,000,000
1900 — $  50,000,000
1910 — $100,000,000
1920 — $250,000,000
1930 — $750,000,000
```

By the time of Woods' death in 1927, his agency had surpassed the majority of life insurance companies in value of policies in force.

The true measure of Woods' importance lies not in his company's success but in the work he did as a leader in NALU to upgrade the education and training of agents.

After the 1906 investigation the immediate need was to restore the public's confidence in life insurance and the agents who sold it. Woods and other NALU leaders started intensive educational and training programs for agents. At the same time, they worked on a program to educate the public about life insurance.

One of the NALU's first orders of business was to put out an official publication that would regularly communicate with all NALU members. In 1906 *Life Association News*, the NALU's official publication, was born.

Six years later, in 1912, the association and 40 of its affiliates founded the industry's first cooperative national life insurance publicity campaign.

Two years later, in 1914, the theme of the entire NALU convention was "Life Insurance Education." The featured speaker was Dr. Solomon S. Huebner, a young professor from the Wharton School of Finance and Commerce at the University of Pennsylvania, who taught the first college-level courses on insurance. Huebner talked about the important and necessary role the life insurance agent played in American society. He stressed the need for an agent to understand his role better so that he could do a better job of selling to a client who was uneducated about life insurance.

Huebner believed that the agent had an almost missionary

task in helping a client to insure himself adequately. Huebner's goal for the agent was to insure a client to the extent that in the event of untimely death, the insurance benefits would approximate the income the client would have earned had he not died.

Huebner's ideas weren't new to top producers like Woods, who had already been conducting their businesses according to similar principles. But for the general NALU membership Huebner's ideas were an exciting stimulant to their minds. The fact that Huebner was an outsider somehow gave added impact to his words.

Huebner presented another idea—that agents who completed a certain level of education in life underwriting should have a professional degree, similar to the CPA designation. Again, it wasn't a new idea. It was the manner in which Huebner presented it that added impetus, that planted the seed more firmly.

Because of Huebner's enthusiastic reception at the convention and his ability to articulate the new ideas that Woods and other top producers had been formulating for years, the education committee of the NALU commissioned Huebner to write the first comprehensive textbook on life insurance marketing.

In retrospect, the situation seems incredible. The selling of life insurance had been going on for more than 70 years; it had grown from a handful of part-timers to a major new industry with combined in-force policies valued in the neighborhood of $20 billion; and the product itself was so misunderstood that it demanded a nationwide education program—yet no one had produced a textbook on the subject!

In fact, publishers at the time were so reluctant to put the book into print that Edward Woods had to guarantee personally any losses that might be incurred by the publisher. Despite this initial lack of enthusiasm, Huebner's book was published in 1915 and was an immediate success. It represented the first milestone in Huebner's close association with the NALU.

Also in 1915, Woods was elected president of the NALU. His leadership provided a new focus for the somewhat random educational and training activities that were taking place around the country and raised the sights of the association to a new level.

Woods was a believer in education and training. He had influenced the Equitable Society to establish its early educational and sales training programs, which he used within his own agency—then the largest of the Equitable.

Woods convinced 15 companies, four of which were in the life insurance business, to form the Bureau of Salesmanship Research, which became affiliated with the Carnegie Institute of Technology.

Woods was concerned that 80 percent of newly licensed agents left the business in their first year and their selection and training were tragically poor. Woods also perceived that proper research was needed to find out exactly what was wrong before corrective educational programs could be devised.

Under Woods' leadership the NALU sponsored the writing of textbooks in addition to Huebner's, thus broadening the base of life insurance literature.

Woods certainly wasn't alone in his efforts, yet he serves as a good example of the enlightened individuals who were beginning to assume leadership roles in the local and national associations—individuals who were volunteering their time and effort to better their occupation.

One man who worked closely with Woods was Winslow Russell, an agency executive of Phoenix Mutual and a member of the Phoenix board. Russell was one of those rare company leaders who saw a need to overhaul the agent's role and did something about it.

In 1913 Russell surveyed his 1,700 agents and discovered that fully 40 percent had not produced a single dollar of new business, another 45 percent had produced very little, and a mere 15 percent of his agents were producing nearly 70 percent of the company's new business.

Armed with this and other information, Russell began a 10-year revamping of Phoenix Mutual's agency structure. He dismissed all part-time agents, who represented 60 percent of his sales force. He standardized agents' contracts and reduced the number of general agencies. Then he began a two-week home office training program for all new agents, coupled with large enough salaries and commissions for the beginning agent to live on. He also set up scholarships for veteran agents who wanted advanced training.

The results? In 1913 Phoenix Mutual's 1,700 agents had produced $21,000,000 in new business. At the end of Russell's revamping program, in 1923, Phoenix Mutual had 375 agents, who produced $52,000,000 in new business.

As a consequence of his 10-year program, Russell accumulated a mass of statistical information that demolished the validity of the old "warm body" concept of getting anyone who wanted to sell out on the streets. In 1923 the average Phoenix agent was better trained, presented a better public image of Phoenix, and, even more important, made a better living for himself than did the earlier untrained, unmotivated agents.

Although the results of Russell's efforts were known throughout the industry, it took years before other companies began to institute similar approaches to their marketing forces. However, the NALU, buoyed by the leadership of individuals like Woods and supported by the results of experiments like Russell's, pushed ahead in its attempts to upgrade the insurance agent.

In 1921 the leaders of the NALU again turned to Huebner. They asked him to help draw up model curricula for life insurance instruction in colleges and secondary schools. Interest was growing in insurance education. The success of the Carnegie School of Practical Insurance Salesmanship, which started in 1919, stimulated the formation of similar divisions at New

York University, Boston University, the University of Denver, and the University of Oklahoma. Most of these schools submitted their proposed curricula to the NALU's Committee on Educational Standards for approval.

In response to the snowballing interest in insurance education programs, in 1926 the committee, working hand in hand with Huebner, published a complete guide for educators to structuring and developing insurance courses. It was a landmark program, called *Outline of Collegiate Courses in Functions, Principles, and Practices of Life Insurance.*

Institutions around the country grabbed it up. It was the most comprehensive document published to that date on how to teach insurance. It represented the hundreds of years of accumulated experience of the top agents who helped put it together.

In the early 1920s a young leader named Paul Clark began to attract attention. Clark was among the first of the new breed of professional agents that all the educational efforts of the NALU had been aimed at producing. He was a graduate of Wharton, where he had studied with Huebner. Clark's uncle, Ernest Clark, was a highly successful general agent and a close associate of Woods. Paul Clark was therefore a product of the finest minds in the insurance business. He was to become one of the greatest leaders in the history of the life insurance business.

In 1924 Huebner again spoke before the NALU convention, and again he stressed the need for a professional designation for the life insurance underwriter. But this time, after 10 years of intensive educational efforts, the concept seemed more realistic, a logical result of the push to educate and upgrade the life insurance underwriter.

Lawyers had degrees. Doctors had degrees. Accountants had degrees. Why not a degree for the qualified, educated individual who played such an important role in securing a person's future? Why not a degree that would let the consumer know when he was dealing with a qualified life underwriter?

Why not, indeed! In 1927, after three years of intensive work with Huebner and with the prodding leadership of Woods and Paul Clark, the NALU authorized the establishment of the American College of Life Underwriters. Thus was launched the educational institution that would provide life insurance and related courses leading to the Chartered Life Underwriter (CLU) professional degree.

After more than 85 years the life insurance industry had finally arrived at a point where an accumulated body of knowledge about the field was available. And an agent, by mastering this knowledge, could be ranked as a professional.

Of course having the knowledge available didn't mean that everyone would take advantage of it. And even earning the degree did not mean that an agent suddenly achieved an exalted status in the eyes of the consumer. In fact, the battles for better education and wider acceptance of the CLU degree are still being fought today.

But the important thing is that finally a structure existed for professionalism. This rapid, agent-initiated push for professionalism took fire after the 1906 Armstrong Investigation and culminated at the 1927 NALU meeting with the founding of the American College of Life Underwriters.

CHAPTER FIVE

A Flock of Eagles

The Million Dollar Round Table started in 1927. What a year that was!

The world was at peace. The economy was growing at a breakneck pace. More people had more money than ever before. It was a time for optimism, especially in the life insurance business, where the value of policies in force had doubled over the 10 years from 1916 to 1926.

The enthusiasm was evident at the National Association of Life Underwriters (NALU) convention held in Memphis in October, 1927, where the members were buoyed up by more than an economy that promised a bright future. They were excited because they had just approved the formation of the American College of Life Underwriters, which was the result of many years of effort to upgrade the education of the agent. The college was a major symbol that the agents were raising their status in the world and had taken a long step toward professionalism.

There was also excitement about a new development at the convention. For the first time the top-producing life insurance agents in the country would meet to exchange ideas in a closed-door session. For the first time the high-flying eagles who were the epitome of life insurance agents would flock together.

The man who provided the impetus for establishing the Million Dollar Round Table was Paul Clark. In addition to being the first president of MDRT, Clark was a founder of the American College of Life Underwriters. Later he became a president of NALU.

After spending his earlier years helping to upgrade the quality of agents, Clark went into management. He eventually became president and chairman of the board of the John Hancock Mutual Life Insurance Company.

But in 1927 most of this was still ahead of Clark. He was 35 years old and was chairman of the program committee for the NALU Convention. It was Clark's idea to get the successful producers together. Although most of the members were excited about the idea, some thought that a meeting of the elite would be a divisive factor within the NALU. And there were some jokes around the convention about the arrival of "knights in shining armor." But Clark supported the exclusive nature of the meeting. In fact, he had named the group "Million Dollar Round Table" to immediately identify its exclusivity.

Clark wanted the top producers to become involved in stronger leadership roles within the association. Many of the top agents weren't even members of the NALU. Also, Clark thought that the ideas of the successful producers would give the convention more substance and inspiration.

But most of all, Clark—being a large-volume producer himself—was keenly aware that the top producers had no place to go to discuss their problems. He knew that many of them had been meeting informally in recent years and had the need for an established forum.

What needs of life insurance agents, and top producers in particular, led to this meeting of minds? First of all, built-in characteristics and weaknesses of the agency system and the job itself required it. The agent was physically removed from the home office and very often from the general agent or manager for whom he worked. In a critical moment with a client there was no one for the agent to turn to. He either sank or swam—alone! Also, it could be a relatively lonely occupation—lonely in the sense that there were few or no peers readily available with whom to share ideas or discuss problems.

The successful producers had special needs that could be satisfied through meeting with their peers. On his way up several things typically happened to a top agent. He sank his roots deeply into a community and built his business on an intimate, person-to-person basis. He usually started out selling policies for personal and family protection, but as his clients' needs grew so did he. He graduated to simple and then complex estate planning, then to working with the various business uses of life insurance, and finally to the writing of employee benefit plans, which involved the use of group life insurance, health and disability insurance, and perhaps annuities. He was plunged into a plethora of insurance applications that required a knowledge of income and estate taxes, trusts, finance and capital formation, business organizations, compensation plans, banking, and more.

As the agent got into these sophisticated areas of financial planning and business uses of life insurance, where could he get help and answers?

The top agent found that the trade journals, company meetings, and local association meetings didn't provide the help he needed, because they dealt with problems faced by the average agent. If the agent turned to his company, general agent, or manager for help, he faced the same impasse—they often didn't have the knowledge or sophistication needed to solve his complex problems.

The growing agent often found himself solving complicated business and estate problems with relatively skimpy information and direction. Frequently he had the gnawing thought:

"Maybe there's a better way to do this . . . a different way that will better protect my client."

Meeting with agents who shared his problems was often the only way to obtain the knowledge or techniques needed. Such expertise wasn't in "the book"—it was in the heads and experiences of the agent's peers.

So there was always a need for the top agents to get together and pick one another's minds for ideas—to share thoughts, to try to find out if there is a "better way." That's the most easily demonstrable reason for the successful agents to assemble.

But there's another, less tangible, reason that is just as important. On his way to the top the agent develops such an enthusiasm for his product that his zeal becomes almost messianic in intensity. Without exception, successful producers have this enthusiasm, and it's not phony. Most of them have delivered enough death claims to know how much their services and policies mean to the survivors, and most of them trace their first feelings of messianic zeal to their first death claim.

So it is equally important for these agents to meet to recharge their enthusiasm. There's a special magic that happens at the Annual Meetings of the successful producers that no one can really define. It's more than just sharing ideas or knowing that others share the same problems. It's the special nod of approval, the sincere compliment, the warm handshake from a peer that gives the agents the extra stimulus, the booster shot, that enables them to go home and excel in their profession for another year.

Back in the 1920s new uses of life insurance for business purposes were growing as rapidly as the United States. More than ever before, the top agents needed to get together to share ideas.

Paul Clark, with the backing of the NALU, wrote to the leading companies for the names of agents who sold over $1,000,000 in policies. The companies were less than enthusiastic, because they feared that such a meeting would expose their highest producing agents to other companies that might be more appealing.

But Clark persisted, and he finally ended up with a list of 72 agents. He invited them all to attend, and 31 showed up. With Clark, the total attendance at the first meeting was 32.

Clark made a rule that lost him some friends, but which established the basic concept of the Round Table—that only producers who had a provable record of a million dollars in sales could attend the meeting. Clark made no exceptions. It was an arbitrary figure, but Clark was adamant in setting a minimum amount that was high enough that the successful producers would know that they were sitting down with their true peers.

The first meeting was a closed luncheon at the Peabody Hotel in Memphis on October 13, 1927. Some of the agents were razzed as they entered the room. But Clark quickly put all criticism to rest with a simple statement that is still a creed for MRDT:

"The thing for those on the outside to do is to increase their production so as to get inside."

The historic session lasted a little over two hours. Sixteen of the 32 gave presentations. A half-hour at the end of the meeting was devoted to a business session during which the group voted to continue the Million Dollar Round Table and determined that it would meet yearly during the NALU convention. The three best presentations were selected by a nonmember panel of guests and were presented to the general assembly. This became a tradition that has continued to the present at each NALU convention.

The most fascinating aspect of this first meeting is that the early members talked about the same general subjects as the members were to discuss in every subsequent meeting of the Round Table.

Several speakers talked about selling from the client's point of view, of putting themselves in the client's shoes, and of using the client's language in a sales presentation. They also talked about the importance of being a good listener in learning a client's wants and needs.

Others explained the various methods they used to get all the information they needed from a prospect in order to prepare a tailor-made proposal. One speaker even handed out copies of the fact-finding form he used to solicit information from a prospect.

Some talked about the need for keeping a proposal simple so that the prospect wasn't overwhelmed with too many facts and figures.

Several mentioned the importance of selling the "living benefits" of life insurance.

One speaker gave a detailed explanation of how he used life insurance to help preserve the estates of his wealthy clients.

Two speakers gave examples of how they used advertising to increase their business.

Another explained how he sold life insurance to clients who owned their own businesses.

Another gave the members ideas on how they could save time and money through office efficiency.

Another talked about the need for a life insurance agent to be well-rounded, to get involved in community affairs.

Certainly the methods of dealing with these topics are more sophisticated today, but the basic concerns are still the same. For example, volumes of material have been presented at the Annual Meetings to attune the agent to the need for putting himself in his client's shoes—selling from the client's point of view. Likewise, much material has since been presented on the methods of prospecting for clients and how to handle fact-finding, on using life insurance to preserve estates, and on the business uses of life insurance.

In more recent times the Round Table has developed in-depth educational programs, some of which took years to complete, that explain how agents can make better use of their time through more efficient office and personal procedures.

And throughout the history of the Round Table the top producers have evinced a concern about the development of life insurance agents as well-rounded individuals. Today, the more personal topics discussed at the Annual Meetings, which deal with the Whole Man Concept, rank with equal importance alongside the business objectives of the meetings.

Just as the basic concerns of the high-volume producers haven't changed, neither has the integrity of these successful agents altered. This integrity was displayed at the first meeting by R. U. Darby when he said: "I tell a man that under no circumstances do I want him to have a dollar's worth of life insurance unless he needs it . . . that my job is more to help him solve his problems and his need rather than to make a sale . . . that I would as truthfully and conscientiously recommend that he do not increase his life insurance as to have him increase it."

This statement neatly paraphrases the pledge that all agents must make before they receive their Chartered Life Underwriter degree.

It's a striking testimonial to that charter group's commitment to upgrading the profession that the very first official act of the Million Dollar Round Table was to endorse the American College of Life Underwriters and to encourage every career agent to study for the CLU designation.

Today nearly 40 percent of all MDRT members are CLU's, and that designation is a requirement for achieving MDRT Qualifying and Life membership. MDRT members, through the Million Dollar Round Table Foundation, also contributed $1.5 million toward the building of the MDRT Foundation Hall, a continuing education center on the campus of the American College of Life Underwriters at Bryn Mawr, Pennsylvania.

The persons who attended the first meeting were encouraged enough by the honest sharing of ideas that they voted to make the group permanent. Within two years the meetings had progressed to the point where formal presentations on subjects of interest to all were assigned before the meetings took place, and the traditions of involvement and commitment that still characterize the Round Table had begun to take root.

The agents who attended the first meetings were powerful, highly motivated individuals, capable people with high hopes and aspirations for themselves in particular and for all agents and the insurance business in general. They believed in what they were doing. They were visionaries who also had the knack of being doers. They made things happen because they believed in what they were doing, and they did it in a manner that has become the trademark of the successful insurance agent—by first being tireless, persistent, and resourceful prospectors, and, secondly, by consistently selling from the client's point of view.

The first meeting of these high flying eagles was small, unsophisticated, and almost innocent in character. But it was because of this simplicity in fulfilling basic needs that the Million Dollar Round Table idea took root and flourished. It was conceived as a meeting of peers at which they could exchange ideas honestly. With remarkably few meanderings up blind alleys the Round Table has remained true to its original purposes and objectives. In view of the monsoon of change that has rocked the world for the past 50 years, this adherence to original goals is not only remarkable but unique.

But whoever said that a flock of eagles would be anything less than unique?

CHAPTER SIX

Catching the Updrafts

The Million Dollar Round Table is without question the most powerful group in the world today for raising the quality of life insurance selling.

To belong is coveted because membership is a symbol of excellence.

Yet only about three percent of life insurance agents qualify for membership.

They come from 35 countries and represent more than 400 life insurance companies.

How can such a relatively small handful of agents set world-wide industry standards?

The answer seems like an oversimplification. It's because of the members. The simple fact is that each member is a leader who has gotten where he is on his own, on his own turf, in his own way. He has set as a goal for himself the only recognized universal standard of life insurance sales performance in the world—membership in MDRT—and he has accomplished that goal many, many times over.

When leaders assemble, they lead. And that's exactly what has happened at the Round Table. In their meticulous, no-

nonsense way these leaders have established an association that is absolutely unparalleled in terms of its impact on its industry.

MDRT is exciting. Why?

The organization is completely run by its members. At first thought this may seem like a ho-hum. It's not.

The committees of the MDRT function on volunteer hard work. Over 1,200 agents take time out from their own selling activities to contribute to one of the many committees that either run the association, plan the Annual Meetings, or establish new educational directives for the future of the profession.

It's not a put-on. There are no honorary committees in the Round Table. Every member of every committee not only volunteers his own time but has to produce work on a specified time schedule.

One day recently the Bylaws Committee was meeting in a conference room. The five agents, who came from all parts of the United States and were taking time out from their own businesses, were wrestling with the problem of whether or not to increase the minimum sales that a person needs to qualify for the MDRT.

At the same time, the five-member Executive Committee, which controls all MDRT activities, was meeting in the President's office. They had a 15-point agenda that covered everything from the policing of membership to the sponsorship of half-time activities at the Liberty Bowl Football Game to a long-range plan for the computerization of all information related to life insurance selling. As usual, their agenda went from the prosaic details of the functioning aspects of the association to some of the most advanced thinking in the entire industry.

These illustrations represent but one small part of one day, but they serve as a perfect example of MDRT's activities, not only because there was so much activity but because it was all member-originated and member-oriented.

The MDRT staff of over 40 professionals is like a tightly wound spring that jumps into action to carry out each directive from the members. And the members are there constantly. In fact, the offices are intentionally located within 10 minutes of the world's busiest airport, Chicago's O'Hare International, to accommodate the many members of committees who flow in and out of the headquarters, often making the round trip in a single day.

MDRT is what an association should be but so few are. In most associations there's such a low level of involvement of the members that the paid staff assumes a large portion of the decision-making role. MDRT is that rare association where members retain a day-to-day involvement in not only the policy decisions but also the administration of the association.

It is axiomatic in association work that no matter how good the paid professionals are their work will at best reflect the vigor and interest of the members. The greater the involvement of the members, the more responsive their association staff will be. At MDRT, because of the intense involvement of its members, the professional work is of the highest quality.

The activity, the membership involvement, the high standards did not happen by accident. Nor did they happen because of the dynamic leadership of a single individual. They happened through a continuity of leadership that has been of a consistently high quality.

The MDRT staff often talks about this high quality of individuals who achieve leadership in MDRT, saying that had members chosen other professions they would be corporate presidents, senators, governors. Of course, the man who started the Round Table, Paul Clark, later became president and chairman of the board of one of the largest insurance companies in the world, the John Hancock. Among others who have become chief executives of life companies are John Hill, president of Aetna Life; Charles Schaaff, former president of Massachusetts Mutual; and Earl Clark, president of Occidental Life.

One past president (1972) of the Round Table, Jim Longley, was elected governor of Maine in 1974, the only politically independent governor in the country. Longley, like most of the top Round Table members, was closely involved in community affairs while he was becoming one of Maine's top-producing agents. So involved, in fact, that a previous governor asked him to head up a study of governmental efficiency. After Longley submitted his report and saw that nothing was being done to implement his group's suggestions, he decided to go ahead and do what few others in the history of United States politics have ever done—achieve major political office without the backing of a major political party.

Jim Longley is not an exception but a dramatic example of the type of individual who rises to leadership in the MDRT. In a way, however, Longley is unique because he ventured out of his profession. Most past leaders of the Round Table remained in the life insurance business.

Even though some had doubts early in their careers, few ultimately decided to change their profession. This singleness of devotion to the career of selling life insurance is especially unusual because so many of the past leaders could have gone the route of Jim Longley. The Past Presidents have had the poise, presence, and ability to speak before audiences and the ability to communicate ideas honestly—all attributes of a successful executive or a respected politician.

Top life insurance agents probably remain in their profession for the same reason they succeed as agents. To get to the top they need to develop a belief in their product and their important role in planning others' lives as well as a devotion to their profession—a devotion that in most cases weds them to their career for life.

But enough generalizations! Here's the straight scoop in brief about the development of MDRT.

The top producers, the eagles, would have nothing less than the finest organization in the world. The Million Dollar Round

Table is the best because it fulfills its members' needs in four critical ways.

It's exclusive.

It produces the finest sales meetings in the world.

It's run by its members.

It produces year-round educational programs that have filled a vacuum in the business lives of the agents.

The members demanded an exclusive club because they needed a forum where they could meet with their peers to exchange sales ideas, to ponder new areas of life insurance involvement that needed cross-pollinization of thoughts, to sharpen sales skills, and to help one another reinforce their belief in their product.

So a lot of the effort of the Round Table over the years has been directed toward the goal of making sure that every member of the association is indeed a peer. This is easier said than done, because there are so many different types of life insurance policies and so many different methods of selling that qualifying for membership in the Round Table has become as complex as income tax forms.

Every annual report includes something related to qualification for the MDRT. The rules governing membership are constantly changing, not to accommodate marginal applicants, but to make sure that the standards remain high. Even today the efforts continue to push the requirements for membership even higher. Even with the number of qualifiers now in the thousands, every effort is made to verify that the applicants have the sales to qualify for membership.

Most professional associations push to increase their membership. This has not been so with the Million Dollar Round Table. It has constantly strived to exclude those who aren't top producers, and never has it solicited new members. The point has been to maintain the MDRT's identity through its exclusivity—to keep it an elite club of only those who could prove a sales record that was acceptable. Even though the membership of the Round Table has soared, this is a reflection of the fact that more agents are becoming more professional rather than that standards have been lowered.

Once the standards are set for qualification, the thrust of the association turns to producing the finest sales meeting in the world.

At first the meetings were simple stand-up-and-talk affairs, but the ingredients were there that were to set the standards for the later meetings. The prime criterion for successful speakers was that they were prepared to talk in specific terms about a field-tested idea that could be transferred to the people in the audience.

The meetings gradually became more complex as each program chairman tried to improve on the preceding program. There were unrelenting pressures on each successive leader to equal and improve on the meetings and always to fulfill the basic needs and expectations of a majority of those who attended. The basic objectives remained the same, but the presentations became more sophisticated. For example, in the early 1950s a meeting of the Round Table featured a professionally staged original drama about the life of an agent.

The Round Table was building a reputation for planning and staging the best down-to-earth, bread-and-butter, meat-and-potatoes inspirational sales meetings in the world.

The Round Table has kept the faith of its members by constantly upgrading its Annual Meeting.

These continuing efforts include the careful selection and definition of subject matter, the close screening and selection of speakers, the peer review and approval in advance of written manuscripts from speakers, the requirement that speakers provide pre-meeting tape recordings, the holding of dress rehearsals for all speakers, and the use of professional direction and every known audio and visual tool.

In summary, the Annual Meetings are the best sales meetings in the world because they are directly responsive to the needs of the members of the association.

The tradition of member involvement started early. All the work involving the Round Table was done by the Presidents of the association for the first 22 years, until 1949, when a permanent office with a paid staff member was opened in Chicago. Even then it wasn't until 1958 that the association hired its first professional manager.

The concern was always that a paid staff wouldn't have the commitment that the members demand. Despite the initial debates over a professional staff, the association grew so quickly that help was needed. The paid staff grew as the need for it expanded. But the tradition of direct member control over the activities of the association persevered, and today the 40-plus members of the professional staff are intertwined with the member committees that direct their activities.

Nothing can illustrate the special involvement of members in the MDRT better than the educational programs devised by the Round Table. For years the agents were faced with problems that they couldn't resolve individually. The only way some of these problems could be handled was through their own group, the Round Table. So the association served to tackle as a group what a person couldn't solve individually.

The first in-depth educational program was devoted to solving the problems of office and personal efficiency. Although this seems like a prosaic theme for such a dynamic organization, the truth is that in over a century of selling the life insurance agent had no educational material that would explain how to organize an office for better efficiency. So the association devised educational programs that would fill many of the vacuums that existed in the knowledge of the agent.

A quick review of an association as diverse as the Round Table can only hit upon the major elements, such as the drive to maintain exclusivity, the production of top-quality sales meetings, the member involvement, and the educational programs. These are mainly results of the highest flying eagles pooling their knowledge.

Directly involved in this history are the agents who made it all happen—the concerned and highly motivated entrepreneurs who gave their time to assure that all agents would have the opportunity to learn from their expertise.

From the beginning the leaders of the Round Table never lost touch with the members. They remained active. There was continuous melding of the old and the new, an unparalleled continuity of giving and sharing. For example, nearly half of those members who attended the second meeting of the Round Table were still active in the association 20 years later.

These past leaders weren't just a bunch of old coots who came to meetings to relive old times. Quite the contrary. They were the tough, hard-nosed breed who had successfully weathered the depression and were willing to share their knowledge with the younger members. They were wealthy, successful people who volunteered their time to the Round Table in an effort to raise the sights and standards of their profession.

Past leaders have set a tradition of continuing involvement that has given the Million Dollar Round Table a continuity of leadership—leadership that has made the difference between mediocrity and excellence, between just getting along and being the best.

So the Round Table evolved from an annual forum, where the top producers could meet with their peers to discuss mutual problems and concerns, into a high-powered organization totally responsive to the needs and wants of its members. It has accomplished this by offering Annual Meetings that are the best in the world and by publishing educational programs that fill basic needs of the agent.

The Million Dollar Round Table is the most effective organization in the world today for upgrading the level of life insurance agents.

CHAPTER SEVEN

The Most Successful Salesmen in the World

The only similarity among Round Table members is their vocation—they sell life insurance. Otherwise, they're like an encyclopedia of birds of the world. The plumage differs. The chatter varies. They achieve flight in different ways.

But make no mistake about it. They all have achieved flight, soaring above others to enter the select circle of the most successful salesmen in the world.

Attend any Round Table function. The differences among the members are so noticeable that you'd think some hotel computer went berserk and scheduled a dozen different groups at the same time. You might see a muscular, bearded young man who looks like he wrestles bears in his spare time with his arm wrapped around a short, bald man wearing a $500 tailored suit. Look to another part of the room and you might find a tall, open-faced back-slapper gladhanding a stern-faced banker type. Turn again and you could see a short, grandfatherly type with a yarmulke perched atop his head talking with a young woman who could pass for an IBM junior executive.

The physical differences go on ad infinitum. A casual by-stander could think of no logical reason for such a disparate group to get together. No reason, that is, until two words are mentioned: "life insurance."

Suddenly the group becomes one. The differences disappear. The mysterious alchemy that bonds the Round Table together takes over. The members, who moments before seemed such a diverse group, now coalesce and become one unit.

The natual tendency of any outsider—especially a young agent hoping to make the Round Table—is to try to categorize these super agents, to find common attributes, similarities in approach, common denominators in their backgrounds.

If a life insurance company had such a profile of MDRT members, it could simply hire new agents who fit the mold and suddenly have an entire force of top producers. But the problem is that each member is as individualistic as his own fingerprint.

It's not that no one has tried to identify the common factors. Over the years, almost from the beginning, so many studies of Round Table members have been made that they could probably paper Grand Central Station.

The studies are interesting. They do tend to draw some basic profiles. They tend to destroy some myths about the profession. But the basic conclusions are really no more than a verbalized salute to the work ethic. As one top producer replied when asked how he got to the top, "I worked my butt off."

Drawing from all the studies, some common elements appear. Round Table members are intelligent self-starters, aggressive yet personable. A high percentage went to college, most of them paying their own way.

Most come from middle-class backgrounds. But here is a good example of how statistics can lead to false generalizations. The top producer of all time started in poverty. Another man, close to the all-time high, came from old-line wealth.

Most entered the life insurance business early in their

careers—but not as a last resort, as the stereotype would have it. To the contrary, most entered the business because they were favorably impressed by another top producer.

Most got to the top by selling a lot of policies to a lot of people, not by selling large policies to wealthy friends.

Most remain loyal to the life insurance company with which they're affiliated and will place policies with other companies only when a client has special needs or wants.

Not surprisingly, most work long hours. The man who makes it to the Round Table in his first four years in the business averages 23 client presentations per week. Working nights and weekends is common, especially among the younger agents.

Most have never thought they would prefer some other occupation. Most prefer their independent, self-employed status as agents to a management job within the life insurance industry. If they had a second-choice career, most say they would have been in medicine or law.

Most work in cities of less than a million population. Most also have clients outside of their own state or province.

Most spend a higher percentage of their income on a continuing self-education program for themselves than do agents not in the Round Table.

Most want their children to go into the life insurance business.

Personality traits of the top producers are predictable:

- "highest self-confidence."
- "sociable, warmhearted . . . but doesn't over-socialize with clients."
- "mentally tough . . . doesn't lose confidence through client indifference, resistance, and put-offs."
- "strong tendencies toward action."
- "thoroughly enjoys influencing people."
- "a hard worker from youth."

- "will pay a much higher price than the average man for the rewards he is seeking."

These are some of the many generalizations that have come out of the studies. Certainly the statistics might help a general agent in recruiting a new agent. But if a general agent relied exclusively on the statistical averages, he would not have hired many of the largest volume producers of all time.

One of the greatest of all life insurance agents doesn't fit any patterns that a general agent might look for. He went from selling poultry and eggs for $10 a week to selling debit life insurance, a type of policy where the agent not only made the sale but once a week went around to his clients and collected a small premium. Even after he became one of the top debit agents in his area, he still had to beg another life insurance company to give him the chance to sell regular life insurance.

His old company predicted that he would fall flat on his face. Even the new company took him on with reluctance. Yet he eventually became one of the largest individual producers in the world, with first-year commissions totalling over $1,000,000 a year.

The life insurance industry has aptitude tests that most companies give to prospective agents to see if they have what it takes to sell. Many successful agents in the Round Table gleefully explain how they flunked the test.

So, as much as the psychologists try to define what personality traits will result in a person being successful at selling life insurance, they haven't been able to come up with a formula that works.

Members themselves aren't much help in defining what it takes to succeed. Generally they're too action-oriented to stop for much introspection. When pinned down, they talk about hard work, organization, goal setting, having an interest in people, dedication—all attributes that even a casual observer would assign to them.

There is no easy answer to the question of what the million-dollar producers have that the run-of-the-mill agents lack.

Although the surveys provide some clues, no generalization could do justice to the tremendous variety of personalities who achieve leadership in the organization.

The first natural assumption is that the top underwriters started with connections of one sort or another, either by being born to wealth or through being privy to some type of inside business dealings.

This theory holds less water than a sieve. Nearly every general agent has his story of the child of wealthy parents who tried to make it as an insurance agent by capitalizing on his parent's friends—and bombed out miserably.

A handful of the top agents were born to wealth. Take the example of one past president, who came from a wealthy family. He was too embarrassed to call on acquaintances, so he did all his prospecting for clients in a nearby town where he wasn't known. A relatively miniscule number of wealthy-born achieved top production, but only after careful preparation and devotion to their careers.

Recent members of the Executive Committee are more typical. Their backgrounds are middle class to lower middle class. One said, "In my family, we wished we had enough money to even be called 'poor.' " By far the vast majority of top producers in the Round Table are self-made.

Some top producers are the offspring of insurance agents. If anyone had connections, these producers did. They were raised in the hard-working lifestyle of the agent. They knew what sort of commitment the vocation demanded. But few were handed anything on a silver platter. Even the offspring of the largest general agents had to pass through a test of fire that was usually more rigorous and demanded more training and education than the general agent demanded of his regular, non-family agents.

In terms of business connections, there are a handful of stories within the industry of agents who were able to capitalize on their insider status. For example, a doctor who examined applicants for a large mutual life insurance company married a fabulously wealthy heiress to a beer fortune. The doctor became a life insurance agent, using in part his wife's money and connections. Eventually he served on the board of directors of 14 of the nation's largest businesses and became a prodigious producer. Working with a Round Table past president, he sold and installed some of the first pension plans for several of the largest manufacturing companies in the country.

Such stories of unusual successes are fun to talk about, but there are no conclusions that can be drawn from them regarding a quick route to success in the selling of life insurance.

A more pungent example comes from another president of the Round Table, who failed in a retail business, then migrated to a Southern city and arrived nearly broke. Impressed with the high income a relative received from selling life insurance, he became an agent himself. The business failure had toughened him—as it usually does anyone who goes through it—but, even more, it gave him an insight into the problems, the dreams, the commitments, and the ego drive that motivate someone who establishes a small business. The new agent had an insider's view of these motivations. He was working in an area where he had absolutely no connections in the traditional sense. He did, however, have connections in the sense that he knew the problems of his clients and was able to empathize with them, and, more important, to write policies that met their needs.

So connections in the traditional sense have had little impact on the top producers' road to success. Once a producer gets to the top, it's a different story, because success begets success the same way that money begets money. When a top agent does a good job for one client, he frequently finds himself writing policies for friends of that client. When the client happens to be a wealthy person or a big business, the referrals are especially meaningful. But that doesn't establish how the top producer got to his top role in the first place.

A popular misconception is that the top producers must come from large metropolitan areas, where there's a plethora of wealthy people and businesses to draw from as clients. But the surveys show that it really doesn't matter. A top producer can just as easily come from a medium-sized town as from a huge metropolis.

A legendary figure in the Round Table who served as its president in 1937 sold life insurance in the Big Horn basin of Wyoming—as unlikely a place for a top producer as anyone could imagine, especially during the depression, when the agent qualified for the Round Table. Once he rode 80 miles round trip, on horseback, to sell a $2,000 policy. During his peak production years there were fewer than 12,000 people within a 50-mile radius of his home. From this unlikely base camp, this agent has been a member of the Round Table for over 45 years.

So connections and location don't seem to matter. What then? Are a significant percentage of top producers affiliated with certain companies? No. Although a particular company may be heavily represented in the Round Table during some periods, its representation is likely to wane during other periods. There's no relationship between the size of a company and the number of agents it has in the Round Table.

What, then, do all the top producers have in common? What makes them different from other agents? What makes them achieve while others either drop out or just piddle along?

Generally top producers are agreeable, intelligent people who listen well. They're so alert to nuances in conversation—probably an acquired talent from having to "read" the thinking of a wide variety of clients—that little escapes them.

The Round Table members are so honest and self-effacing in their dealings with one another that it's not uncommon to find one of them relating a personal story about his own family or telling a story about how dumb he was in a certain business dealing—all in front of a large audience. They admit to their own business and personal failings so candidly that it would astonish a bystander.

Each top underwriter has developed his own methods of prospecting for clients, presenting himself to them, and closing a sale. The techniques vary all the way from a P. T. Barnum approach to a more sedate tape of presentation.

Interestingly, every member feels that his techniques and methods can be improved. Round Table members are always looking for a better, more efficient way. This is probably why more time has been spent at Annual Meetings on prospecting, preparing for, and closing a sale than on any other topic. At the 1966 Annual Meeting one of the largest producers of all time addressed the members for two hours on how he closes a sale. The 1,800 members present hung on his every word and deluged him afterward with requests for more details. Yet later in the same meeting, while another speaker was explaining his closing techniques, the first speaker was taking copious notes.

Despite the differences in technique and approach, one common thread weaves through every top producer's dealings with his clients—selling from the client's point of view.

This ability to empathize, to put oneself in the client's shoes, to sell not only to a client's wants but to his projected needs, is undoubtedly the most important common denominator in all the top underwriters' approaches.

The super salesmen have the ability to empathize with a client. Speakers at every annual meeting have mentioned this as the key to success. It's an intangible part of the chemistry of a sale that requires a belief in the product, a sure-footed knowledge of how the product can be applied to the individual needs of the client, and the missionary zeal to want to make the client "see the light." Evangelistic as this sounds, the top producers have this empathy, sometimes to the point of forgetting that they aren't the client.

"I know at this moment you think I'm a pest," one top producer told a prospect, "but I don't care what you think of me at this moment. I care about what you or your family will think of me twenty years from now!"

The oft-repeated admonition among members of the Round Table is: "Don't try to sell anyone a policy that you wouldn't buy under the same circumstances." To prove the point, members carry a full house of life insurance on themselves.

Another characteristic of the top underwriter is an ability to handle the negative aspects of his business. Many of the top producers have talked about the need for developing a mental toughness that enabled them to deal with client indifference, put-offs, and turn-downs and with many of the negative stereotypes that the average person still has of the life insurance agent.

From learning to deal with these negatives and probably from a greater understanding of the importance of his product, the successful producer develops an optimism about his role in life that allows him to roll with the punches. For example, in the midst of the Depression members attending the 1934 Annual Meeting were predicting a spectacular year for 1935. That's optimism!

More recently a top producer in the Round Table battled for 11 years to secure legislation that would allow professionals to incorporate and thereby obtain the same tax deductions for pension and profit sharing plans and group insurance as other corporations. In pursuit of this goal, he lobbied in his state legislature and in the federal congress, wrote articles, and traveled around the country giving speeches, spending up to 20 percent of his time in some years and investing tens of thousands of dollars. That takes more than mental toughness, it takes optimism. In this case the optimism paid off.

Even on a day-to-day basis, no matter how disciplined an agent is he needs the energy that comes from optimism to catapult him into the day's activities—to turn him from a methodical, organized person into a communicating and convincing evangelist for his product where there is a need for it.

The final common denominator is also extremely important: self improvement.

All the top agents invest large percentages of their incomes in themselves. Part of the investment goes toward material goods that help their office and personal efficiency—items such as dictating equipment, tools to prepare effective visual presentations, or maybe even computer hookups to handle client requests more quickly.

But most of the investment goes into the continuing education of the agents themselves. The process never stops. Even when they have reached the highest pinnacles of selling, the top producers spend upward of 10 percent of their time attending classes, institutes, seminars, study group meetings, and conferences.

Of course, just being well educated and well-informed doesn't automatically turn an agent into a top producer. Nearly everyone in the Round Table can point to an example of someone who has the highest degrees and a great in-depth knowledge of the life insurance business, but who can't sell turkeys on Thanksgiving.

Early in their careers the successful producers established patterns of continuing educational growth, often at great personal sacrifice. When they first started in the business, most were writing simple policies on the lives of individuals. The more they learned, the more they saw that they needed to learn. At the same time their clients were getting more wealthy and developing more complex financial needs. Whereas at first the agent needed simply a knowledge of his product, as his clients' needs expanded he found that he needed to exercise more judgment in selecting the right types of policies in the right amounts and fitting them together so that they would balance the other assets in a client's estate. And the more judgment he was required to exercise, the greater was the agent's need for more information. So the top life insurance agents hunger for knowledge and better selling skills the way other groups of salespeople lust after more tangible objects.

One of the results of this desire for self-improvement is the Million Dollar Round Table. This was why the top producers got together in the first place—to learn from one another. The same desire has pushed the educational efforts of the Round Table to new heights.

The unique breed of human beings who are the top underwriters of life insurance in the world did not arrive at their position by chance. They are tremendously self-willed individuals who believe that hard, well planned work will bring success. They have combined an almost instinctive empathy for their clients with a sophisticated knowledge of their product, which they present with an honest zeal. And they have combined these qualities and achievements with an optimistic view of their role in the world to arrive at that pinnacle where they are justly called the most successful salesmen in the world.

CHAPTER EIGHT

A Gathering of Eagles

Eagles wouldn't gather for anything less than the finest show on earth.

And that's what they get.

Once a year the Million Dollar Round Table puts on the finest sales meeting in the world.

Every agent who aspires to the top levels of his profession wants to qualify for the Round Table and attend its Annual Meetings. The agents know that nothing else will better assist them in that career.

Why?

Because the Million Dollar Round Table's Annual Meeting is total involvement for 24 hours a day for five straight days.

Because it's mass enthusiasm so intense that grown men and women openly weep during some presentations.

Because it's an honest sharing of sales ideas unlike anything found in any other industry.

Because it provides the stimulus of meeting new personalities with original ideas from all parts of the world.

Because it's the group therapy that comes from joining hands and minds with peers to resolve common problems.

What else is it?

". . . the most tremendous upgrading influence of my life."

". . . the turning point in my career."

". . . the most exciting and rewarding five days of my business life."

Such testimonials sound like empty puffery, but the fact remains that no events have had more lifelong impact on more life insurance agents than have the Annual Meetings of the Million Dollar Round Table.

What is it about this meeting that turns good producers into super producers . . . that turns agents' attitudes toward their job from a mere business interest into a professional commitment . . . that uplifts an individual's personal image so that he can admit to the world that he's a life insurance agent?

The greatest contributing factor to the almost magical properties of the Million Dollar Round Table's Annual Meetings is that every person there has earned the right to be there. Only three percent of all agents qualify for membership in the Round Table. So everyone at the meeting is part of an elite group, an aristocracy of the most successful agents in the life insurance business—and the world.

Also, life insurance agents spend their business lives working with the problems and dreams, the joys and sorrows, the accomplishments and defeats of their clients. There's little room to discuss their own ups and downs. At MDRT they're suddenly surrounded by hundreds of others who understand what it feels like to work on a proposal and get a "no," who can comprehend the joy of insuring a child's education or the sorrow of delivering a death claim check or the indignation of being treated like a peddler.

In short, they're surrounded by peers. And they're not talking about someone else's problems and challenges, they're talking about their own. They can express their ideas, their fears, and their goals because the others understand.

And above all, at MDRT they can learn from their peers.

By nature, the top producers are always looking for better ways to do their job. At the meeting they don't just read about a sales technique, they actually listen in person to one of the legendary agents tell how he sold over $100 million the previous year . . . .

. . . or hear a specialist talk about the meaning of a new Internal Revenue Service ruling . . . .

. . . or have breakfast with an expert on pension plans . . . .

. . . or participate in a workshop discussion to learn more efficient ways of operating an office . . . .

. . . or join a room-hopping session about techniques for developing new clients.

Each Annual Meeting is carefully planned by members of the Round Table to make sure that every topic of concern to the agent is covered as completely as possible. Before each meeting enormous planning goes on by volunteer committees. The fact that it's planned by agents who understand the wants and needs of their peers makes the difference between the Round Table meeting and just another convention.

Speakers must submit their presentations to a manuscript review committee of their peers, which may insist on rewrite after rewrite to make sure that each speech communicates what it's supposed to. And even before speakers go through three or four rewrites, they still must submit tape recordings of their initial manuscripts. And that isn't the end of it. Just before the meeting starts, speakers must rehearse their presentations before MDRT members who bear the responsibility for each speech.

Most speakers submit to this intensive review because they know that their goal and that of the review committee is the same—the most informative and interesting speech possible.

At least 90 percent of the speakers are Round Table members. It's regarded as such an honor to address the meeting that even accomplished speakers will spend upward of 100 hours on their presentations to help guarantee a positive reception. One man practiced his speech so often in front of his family that even his children knew it by heart. The point is that everything possible is done to assure that no speaker wastes the valuable time of the agents in the audience.

This type of commitment to excellence infuses every aspect of the meeting. For example, the day before the meeting starts a special task force of members, all wearing straw hats, is at the airport and in the lobby of each hotel to smooth out transportation and hotel problems. During the meeting these "straw hats" direct traffic in and out of the main auditorium and workshop rooms and handle any nitty-gritty problems that may come up.

Another task force handles registration, passing out the meeting kits and identification badges and generally making the members' arrivals as friendly and expedient as possible.

Another group of volunteers provides VIP treatment for special guest speakers, meeting them at the airport with chauffered limousines, getting them checked into their hotel suites, and handling the extra details like a fruit bowl for the room—all done in an effort to make sure that these famous people will never forget their experience with members of the Round Table.

Other volunteers, over 800 in number, work behind the scenes to insure that every detail of the meeting goes off without a hitch. A typical meeting might find . . .

. . . one internationally-known agent directing a stagehand, telling him when to open and close the curtain . . .

. . . a producer who makes over $250,000 a year emptying ashtrays and moving chairs in a meeting room . . .

. . . an insurance company's number one agent running for water for a speaker practicing at the podium . . .

. . . another agent helping to set up microphones to record a speaker.

These are but a few typical scenes that illustrate the massive attention to detail and the commitment to excellence by everyone involved. And at least 20 percent of everyone attending an Annual Meeting does work on one of the task forces.

An Annual Meeting operates on several levels, from the formal, staged presentations with everyone in attendance to the specialized, structured seminars to the relatively unstructured room-hopping sessions to the totally unstructured bull sessions that the agents are encouraged to set up on their own.

For sheer pageantry and emotional involvement, nothing can compete with the formal presentations on the main platform. Every meeting opens with an international flag ceremony. The members from each country stand as their national flag is carried in, starting with the country with the fewest representatives and proceeding to the largest group.

Emotions build as first the smaller groups from countries like Guatemala and the Cayman Islands stand up . . . then the larger contingents from Israel, South Africa, Japan, United Kingdom and Australia rise . . . until the second largest group, the Canadians, stand . . . and, finally, there is a massive rustling as the group from the United States rises.

Main platform presentations are as diverse as they are effective. One speaker might use sophisticated multi-image and rear-screen visuals. The next might stand on a riser in the middle of the audience under a single spotlight. Another presentation might feature two speakers alternating in a rapid-fire dialogue. Some programs have even included original dramas performed with the polish of a Broadway play.

The closing day might feature a prominent musical group such as the Mormon Tabernacle Choir, the Boston "Pops" Orchestra, or the Atlanta Symphony Orchestra. Or the meeting might close with a speaker telling an intensely moving inspirational story.

77

Between the opening flag ceremony and the closing, the agents hear and discuss so many ideas on such an intense schedule that by the time the meeting ends they're physically, intellectually, and emotionally drained. In fact, there's so much to learn that newcomers are warned not to try to put everything they learn into immediate use once they get home.

Because the meeting can be so mind-boggling, the first-timers get special attention. Months before the meeting a veteran member is assigned to each new person to act as an advisor and to do whatever handholding might be necessary until the first-timer gets acclimated.

At each meeting Past Presidents of the Round Table circulate among newcomers at a special orientation session that is conducted before the regular sessions start.

This special care is important because Round Table members know they'll never get a second chance to make a first impression on the newcomers. The old-timers can recall how important their first meeting was to them, and they go out of their way to guarantee that the first meeting of every agent is just as memorable.

Often an agent's first meeting is more than memorable. Many have said it was the turning point of their career. The excitement and involvement begins the minute the agent steps off his plane and is greeted by the "straw-hat" expediters. The agent is whisked to his hotel, where he's greeted by a band, made up of Round Table members, that jazzes it up while the agents are registered in. Other members are there to make sure that nothing goes awry, that all questions are answered, and that every attendee gets settled as quickly as possible.

The night before the opening ceremonies the corridors of the hotels are filled with agents renewing old acquaintances and striking up new ones. Generally the agents go out of their way to associate with agents from other companies to get a greater cross-pollinization of ideas. (They can talk to their own company's agents at company-sponsored meetings.) The evening is friendly, relaxed, filled with laughter, and supercharged throughout with excited anticipation of the days that will follow.

As the sun rises on the morning of the first session, the streets around the hotels are filled with hundreds of agents out jogging, while others are swimming laps in the hotels' pools. The restaurants are packed with early risers who continue the table-hopping and greetings from the night before. Most get to the meetingplace early in an effort to get the best seats for the opening session.

The excitement and drama build until finally the lights go down and the traditional ceremony of the flags begins. As that ends, the President of the Round Table is introduced. The audience jumps to its feet for a thunderous ovation—one of the most emotional moments in the life of every President—and from that moment on every agent is swept up in the drama, the learning and sharing, the stimulating ideas that are all part of the action-packed days to come.

The agents have so much to do that they're literally running from sunrise until late at night. The pace is so intense that most persons probably couldn't last, physically, mentally, or emotionally, for even one additional day.

Few agents find time to go out on the town or even to enjoy the sights of the city where the meeting is held, because there's simply too much to learn and too little time to learn it. The most popular workshops are videotaped so that an agent who attends one can return in the evening to view the one that was held concurrently. All the formal sessions, from the main platform to the workshops are tape recorded, and within hours of its occurrence agents can purchase a cassette or manuscript of any presentation of interest. So even after the formal sessions have ended for the day the agents may still be reviewing the day's activities by watching videotapes, reading manuscripts, or listening to cassettes.

The schedule doesn't leave much time for socializing in the

traditional sense. Agents will meet for breakfast or dinner, but even then they're nearly always picking one another's brains, sharing ideas. Bull sessions that go late into the night consist of more of the same seeking and giving of new thoughts. In fact, there is so little time for carousing and drinking it up—activities that are so much a part of regular major conventions—that hotels have complained to the Round Table that their bar sales were far below their expectations.

Spouses and families of the agents are not allowed at the meetings, except when they're held outside of the continental boundaries of the United States. One reason for this is space limitations at the hotels. But the major reason is that the Round Table knows from experience that once an agent gets swept up in the whirlwind of activities, nothing should slow him down. Also, the informal gatherings at meals and the late hour bull sessions are just as important to the membership as the formal presentations.

One of the many interesting side aspects of the Annual Meeting is the business and personal relationships that develop from acquaintances made there. Younger agents are encouraged to set up study groups with other Round Table members, to meet throughout the year. These are groups of from about five to 25 agents, usually around the same age, who discuss their problems with one another. One study group has held together for more than 40 years. Another includes 10 Past Presidents of the Round Table. The point of a study group is to expand on the camaraderie and ideas that are developed during the Annual Meeting, to make the agents realize that they have a shared destiny. So the study groups, which are formed from associations made during an Annual Meeting, promote lifelong friendships and opportunities to continue growing through a constant, year-round sharing of ideas.

One evening during the Annual Meeting is usually set aside as a talent night, when members perform. The Round Table has many former professional entertainers among its members, so these evenings feature several polished performances. The MDRT Dixieland Band, made up of MDRT members, is always there with its many accomplished musicians. In fact, one recent meeting featured one of the legendary top producers on saxophone and the president of one of the world's largest insurance companies on trombone. Nearly everyone picks up the spirit of the meeting.

Famous guest speakers have been stunned by the standing up-applauding-cheering-stomping receptions given them by Round Table members. John Gardner, the former U.S. Secretary of Health, Education and Welfare, met a President of the Round Table on an airplane two years after Gardner's presentation at an Annual Meeting. Gardner told the President that he had never in his years of speaking encountered an audience as enthusiastic or as responsive as he had at the Round Table, and he added that within a short time after his speech he had received dozens of letters from Round Table members who were finding ways to implement the ideas that Gardner had presented.

Without question, the most memorable parts of each Annual Meeting are the motivational and inspirational presentations made to the entire group. This is where the agents get booster shots for their messianic zeal, where they get the stimulus that reinforces their belief in their product and provides the reason for the intensive hard work and idea sharing that go on during the rest of the meeting. In fact, the agents who come from countries other than the United States or Canada attend mostly for the motivational parts of the meetings, because the business sessions so often deal with selling situations that are indigenous to the United States.

The motivation and inspiration come from a variety of sources. One successful agent brought the wife and son of a deceased client to the meeting. In a major audiovisual presentation on the main platform the three of them explained in detail how the dead man's estate, which was conservatively estimated at

$20 million at the time of his death, was completely wiped out by creditors and taxes. The man hadn't taken the time to sign up for the estate preservation plan that the agent had prepared. Instead, the only thing left for the widow that the government couldn't get its hands on was a small life insurance policy. The survivors explained to the audience how the money from the life insurance had allowed them to live a respectable life and, in the case of the son, obtain an education. Without the life insurance they would have been impoverished. From a $20 million estate to nothing . . . except for life insurance.

The audience became so involved in this story and the agents empathized so much with the problems faced by the survivors that at least half of those in the audience were openly crying. Most top agents have such a total dedication to the belief that life insurance can accomplish future financial security that they become totally immersed in a story that justifies that belief.

Other types of inspirational stories come from members who were able to succeed despite great adversity. One man went from a concentration camp to become a top producer. Another told how he was able to continue his career despite the debilitating effects of multiple sclerosis. Another told how fellow agents had managed his accounts for him when he was struck down by a major illness. Generally, these are tremendously personal stories told straight from the shoulder. The members respond because they can relate to the stories in that they've been through it themselves, perhaps not under such dramatic circumstances as many of the speakers, but to the point that they can understand the challenges and the disappointments, the gratifications and the sorrows that the speakers are relating.

Speakers from outside the life insurance industry are carefully selected for the motivational content of their messages. Over the years some of the speakers have had lasting impact. For example, in the mid-1960s an expert spoke on the need for physical conditioning. As a direct result, hundreds of agents who heard that talk are still involved in daily exercise programs.

Most of the outside speakers' topics are such that the impact is not readily demonstrable. However, that doesn't mean that the speakers were any less effective. Agents will often talk about a speech given by an outsider as many as 15 years before, remembering the content of the speech and relating the impact it had on that member's life.

Of course, no speaker at an Annual Meeting has the drawing power of one of the legendary producers. Within the industry is a handful of agents whose names are household words because these agents have sold such huge amounts of life insurance. When one of these agents appears on the podium, nearly everyone takes notes as if some oracle were telling the key to its magical powers. Even afterward, when one of these agents walks down a hall or through a hotel lobby, he's like the Pied Piper, constantly attracting clusters of agents around him.

As each Annual Meeting comes to a close and most agents are heading back to their homes, a small cluster of other agents is meeting behind the scenes to compare notes. This is the group that will be responsible for the next year's meeting. And already the pressure for them to put on a better show than the one they've just seen is beginning. The responsibilities are enormous, because even though the Round Table has other activities throughout the year, the Annual Meeting is the fountainhead where everything comes together. The challenge is to produce a meeting that is more educational, more motivating, and more inspiring than the meeting just past, and to make sure above all else that it runs with computer-like precision. That each Annual Meeting is usually better than the previous one is a tribute to an organizational structure within the Round Table that provides a continuity of leadership and also to the fervent desire of the agents to make sure that their meeting is as responsive as possible to the needs of their peers.

No one who attends an Annual Meeting ever forgets the experience. One of the most fascinating qualities of the Annual Meetings is that they are always more than the sum of their parts, and no one can really explain why. All who attend realize that they're being swept up in a special, magical, rarefied atmosphere of learning and sharing where all their senses are attuned to higher pitch than ever before . . . where their emotions run at a fevered pace . . . where their mind captures moments that suddenly enlighten their world and put a new perspective on their career . . . where they find new depths of understanding of themselves, their self-images, their self-esteem . . . where they find themselves making commitments they never knew they would make: commitments to themselves, to their occupation, to new friends, and, above all, a commitment to excellence.

For those who qualify for the Round Table the annual gathering of eagles is an unparalleled opportunity to become involved in the finest sales meeting in the world.

CHAPTER NINE

Self-Image

"Wouldn't it be nice if my life insurance agent called today?"

A lot of survivors wish that the deceased breadwinner had had such an attitude. But the truth is that the life insurance agent, especially when he first starts selling, has a variety of negative attitudes to overcome.

Some of the negative attitudes are directed at the product. First, most people associate life insurance with their own death— not the most pleasant subject for prospects to contemplate.

Second, life insurance is not a product that gives immediate gratification. A prospect can't take life insurance for a test drive. He can't feel it, eat it, turn it on, or take it to bed. Only in the abstract does it give him pleasure, and even then only after a good agent has painted a complete mental picture of the implications of what the prospect is accomplishing by buying life insurance.

Some of the negative attitudes are directed at the life insurance agents themselves. Too many incompetent agents have flapped their wings trying to lay a golden egg and instead have left mental deposits of dirt that the good agents have to clean up.

These negative attitudes make it easy for a prospect to say "no." And the "no's" are the "slings and arrows of outrageous fortune" that harpoon the egos of the life insurance underwriters, often even driving them out of the business.

The top producers have had to learn how to deal with the negative attitudes through a maturing process that continues even when they reach the top. Too often the road to maturity is unnecessarily arduous because the younger agents don't come to grips with their own self-image.

The published *Proceedings* of Round Table meetings are replete with example after example of agents explaining how they have grappled with the problems of self-identity.

There's no question that maintaining a positive self-image becomes easier with time. In the beginning a young agent sells small policies to young, lower-income prospects who have little understanding of the importance of the product to their financial future, and who tend to treat the agent as a peddler rather than a financial planner.

So the beginning agent is trying to sell to the type of prospect who is most likely to reject him at a time when he doesn't have the sales know-how or the conviction in his product that the seasoned professionals use to overcome negative attitudes. This is also the period when he hears the immature homilies about life insurance, like:

"I'm insurance poor!"

"Life insurance keeps you poor all your life so that you can die wealthy."

"I'm worth more dead than alive."

"I don't like betting someone that I'm going to die."

As the result of constant rebuffs many young agents develop what's known as "call-reluctance." If they don't make a call, they may reason, they don't risk having another harpoon thrown at their egos.

Some agents may counter early slumps by making a great number of calls. Life insurance companies figured out a long time ago that if an agent made a certain number of calls with a memorized type of presentation, statistics dictated that he would make enough sales to eke out a living.

Every young agent knows this. Company literature stresses it. The general agent reinforces it. But it's not professional selling; it doesn't fulfill a client's wants and needs; and, in the long run, it isn't very rewarding.

The top producers handled their early "call- reluctance" in a variety of ways. Some are so naturally gregarious and warm that they worked within a wide range of personal contacts—through their churches, temples, alumni groups—where prospecting was on a more friendly level and a "no" was never quite as final or hard-lined as when prospecting in the cold. Of course, this is almost the stereotype of the insurance salesman—the friendly backslapper who uses social contacts for business purposes. Generally, however, even the gregarious types, as effective as their casual and relaxed approach may seem in a face-to-face meeting, learned quickly that their smiles meant little without a hard-working, organized schedule and a good knowledge of their product.

Nearly all the top producers learned early that they had to set minimum goals for themselves that would force them to make a certain number of calls each day, no matter how many hours they had to work to meet their goals.

At the same time, they learned more about their product and the sales process to help them counter resistance. This learning process involved more than just reading sales literature or attending seminars or studying for the Chartered Life Underwriter designation. Usually it meant working with a seasoned professional—an experienced agent who enjoyed sharing his experience with the novice.

Most of the top producers can name specific underwriters who steered their careers along. One of the all-time greats in the business even moved from Minneapolis to Buffalo as a young man simply to learn more about the business from a great agent who was regarded as one of the best in the country. What started as a seven-week learning experience turned into a two-year stay.

So as young agents the top producers dealt with their self-image problems by consulting with old-timers, by building their own confidence through knowledge of the product and their own ability to handle sales resistance, and by working long hours to meet the goals they set for themselves. The largest producers often mention discipline as the single idea to which they attribute their early successes. When referred to by top producers, discipline usually encompasses:

- being able to set a schedule and stick to it;
- setting daily, weekly, monthly, and yearly goals;
- working long hours;
- sacrificing leisure time and many personal enjoyments;
- investing money in their continuing education.

Of course, just enumerating the qualities that lead to success, which could apply to nearly every vocation, hardly explains the doubts and fears, the sleepless nights worrying about a big presentation, the tremendous efforts to push harder during down periods. Nor does it explain the many joys that come with accomplishing something on one's own . . . of not only making a big or difficult sale, but knowing that a prospect understands the role life insurance can play in his life . . . the many pleasures of exceeding a goal . . . or the intangible warmth of self-esteem that comes from surpassing the sales of other underwriters in an agency.

Life insurance agents probably have more highs and lows than workers in most other professions because they have to face a wider variety of emotions on a daily basis than most others do. Psychologists have pointed out that our modern society tends to homogenize emotions by encouraging persons to isolate themselves in environments where outbursts of tremendous joy or unremitted sadness are seldom seen and certainly not encouraged. This isolation creates people who are capable of little compassion and empathy for their fellow human beings.

The agent is hardly isolated. One hour he may be writing a policy for the happy parents of a newborn child to cover the baby's future college education, and the next hour he may be attending the funeral of a beloved client. Days later, with mixed emotions, he may bring a large check to the bereaved widow of his client. And twenty years later he may attend the college graduation of the now grown child, knowing that the policy he sold at the child's birth made the college education possible.

Usually the extremes aren't that obvious. But the emotional highs and lows the agent deals with on a daily basis probably account for the sensitivity of the top producers.

This increasing sensitivity brings with it an improved self-image, belf-image, because it helps the agent realize the importance of his work in fulfilling a client's dreams and in protecting the survivors in the event of a disaster.

A limited success in selling builds confidence and brings with it an optimism that makes it easier to handle the "no's" and rebuffs.

Even when they experienced early success, most of the top producers went through periods when they called themselves "financial consultants," "estate planners," or some other title with a more positive image. This usually happened after the agents had been in the business for a number of years, had spent three to five years studying for their Chartered Life Underwriter (CLU) designation and could handle most of their sales without the need of old-timers or specialists to help them close.

Often these attempts to grapple with self-image caused the agent's business to suffer. Some agents fell prey to the tendency to slack off, to say to the world, "Now I have the education and training, so come and see me." One Past President said, "I soon became the lowest paid highbrow consultant in town."

The point that most top producers make about this period in their lives is that they were using a title to demand the type of respect that a banker or lawyer or other professional is accorded. The reality was that they were still regarded as life insurance agents and were given respect according to the professionalism of their work.

Most of the top producers soon learned that they didn't need the titles, that they didn't have to overcome the negative stereotypes of the life insurance agent through the use of a euphemism that obscured the fact that they were life insurance agents. They learned that they received the respect they sought by simply doing a superlative job of planning the financial futures of their clients.

"I don't think much of life insurance agents, but *my* agent is different!"

This statement, which everyone in the business has heard many times, underlines the individualistic, face-to-face, personalized type of business the agent conducts. He doesn't need to battle negative stereotypes as long as he has clients who believe in him, respect him, continue to use his services, and refer him to friends.

As an agent grows, he gradually gets into more complex estate and business financial planning, which helps to boost his self-image. He also becomes increasingly selective in choosing his prospects.

While it is true that some life insurance agents gravitate to wealthy clients, with whom they can use their sophisticated knowledge, there are others who effectively serve the middle and low income brackets.

Many MDRT members are intrigued by the challenge of serving large numbers of clients. They accomplish this through selling union or corporate pension and profit sharing plans, group life insurance plans, or group health and disability plans. Other large markets include life insurance and health insurance sold through salary savings plans sponsored by businesses and industrial firms.

Of course, an agent's self-image has a lot to do with how successfully he can deal with the more erudite prospect. If he acts like a peddler, then that's how he will be treated. But if he takes the stance that he's a professional and can back it up with a knowledge of and enthusiasm for his product, then he will be treated like a professional.

The top producers delight in demanding that their prospects and clients treat them as professionals. Of course they want to make each sale, but they know that they don't need to make every sale to survive. So they can take a position in a given sales situation that they might have thought twice about during their struggling years.

For example, one top producer will simply pack up his briefcase and leave when a prospect isn't giving him full disclosure of financial information. "You wouldn't ask a doctor to diagnose your physical well-being without giving him all the facts. How can you expect me to diagnose your financial well-being without giving me all the facts?" he reasons. This agent takes the stance that he's a proven professional who can't do a proper job unless he gets all the information necessary to do a complete job.

An agent can only assume this stance from a position of strength. He can't be so hungry for a sale that he'll settle for less and take the proverbial "bird in the hand." Rather, he must believe so completely in his product and have so much confidence in his own ability to adapt the product so that it applies to the specific financial needs of the client that he won't settle for less than a full disclosure.

In effect, he's saying: I'm a busy professional. I offer the valuable contribution of my learned mind and my years of experience to the development of your estate. If you have too little respect for me and the product I'm selling to cooperate, then I don't want to waste my time with you."

The self-esteem that is characteristic of the top producers and their belief in their product are infectious intangibles that definitely alter the chemistry of a sale. It is clear that the sooner an agent gets to the level where he can assume this professional stance the sooner he achieves higher production levels and the fewer problems he has with his self-image.

This point is brought home even more clearly by a group of young agents in the Round Table—in their 30s—whose production astounds even many of the old-timers. Several of them began planning for a life insurance career during their early days in college. At least one even got a law degree for the express purpose of forwarding his professionalism in life insurance selling. So some of them have a higher level of preparedness than most starting agents.

In talking to these young successes one thing becomes immediately clear; they have a crisp image of their role as professional life insurance agents. "I'm the best life insurance agent in this town and I don't make any bones about it," one said.

These young agents came to grips with their self-image early in their careers. As all top underwriters have learned to do, they have no qualms about clearly identifying themselves as life insurance agents. They state what they are and demand to be accepted as professionals.

The road to the top is never easy in any profession, but it's particularly difficult for a life insurance underwriter to succeed, with the negatives that swirl about him, until he has the self-confidence and self-esteem to stick out his chest, ruffle up his feathers, and announce to the world:

"I am a life insurance agent, and I'm proud of it!"

CHAPTER TEN

Build a Better Nest

True story:

Along the banks of the Snake River in the Jackson Hole region of Wyoming lived an eagle. As eagles do, this one had marked off his territory. He lived quite comfortably within his domain.

The eagle's nest was near the top of a tree. Naturalists noticed that the nest kept getting bigger and messier. Finally, as the eagle was landing one day, his nest crashed to the earth, and the eagle was injured. The crippled bird soon lost his territory to a younger, stronger eagle and was last seen rummaging around in a much less desirable location.

Moral: *Build a better nest.*

For years life insurance agents have heard that moral, because as high as they may fly they still need a well-organized nest to land in. In fact, without a firmly structured home base an agent will be just as crippled as the eagle in the story.

Yet, as astounding as it may seem, the agency system was a century and a quarter old before anyone developed systematized educational literature to tell the agent how to build a better nest.

The office needs of a life insurance agent are not conceptually any more complex than those of many other small businesses. The key is to develop systems that are simple to manage so that the agent doesn't have to spend valuable time piddling around with the considerable paperwork and records that he's forced to keep.

Without question, the efficiency of the agent's office relates directly to his sales. An efficiently run office gives the agent more time—time to more intelligently select and approach his prospects, time to put that extra touch on a sales presentation, time to serve his old clients better.

A well-run office is not as easy to achieve as it might seem. The busy agent has so many immediate and detailed needs—needs that relate directly to sales that require immediate attention daily—that it's easy to ignore or do a slipshod job with the paperwork, accounting and filing.

Only later, when the agent can't locate an article on some phase of tax law that could make the difference between making or not making a sale . . .

. . . or when he belatedly discovers that a prospect didn't show up for a medical exam . . .

. . . or when he spends extra hours writing up a proposal because he couldn't find the standardized paragraphs that he usually inserts . . .

. . . or when he goes out on too many interviews with unqualified prospects . . .

. . . or when he discovers, too late, that because of poor accounting and poor financial controls his office costs are putting him in debt . . .

. . . that's when he realizes that his nest is disintegrating.

In a poorly run operation the agent is always playing catch-up, not only creating undue mental strain but, more important, taking time from his selling activities. And the only time he's making money is when he's in front of a qualified prospect.

Every person in the life insurance business has witnessed the failure of otherwise excellent agents who couldn't get organized.

In 1964 the Round Table recognized that one of the most valuable services it could provide its members was to help them build a better nest.

The Annual Meeting could provide stimulus and motivation, a sharing of ideas for better presentations and new markets, a recharging of the missionary zeal—but if the agent went back home to an inefficient operation, the learning experience was useless.

So in 1965 a group of high-powered top producers—many of whom would later become Presidents of the Round Table—developed the first comprehensive set of personal and office efficiency manuals in the history of the life insurance business. They gathered their information by doing what top agents have always done—by going to other top agents and asking them to share their ideas. Hundreds of years worth of time-saving ideas and procedural systems were sifted through, organized, and collated into this first manual.

The response was overwhelming! It was like the gold rush, the opening of the Panama Canal, the first rocket to the moon.

The vacuum that existed for this type of manual was so great that agents and life insurance companies from around the world grabbed up copies.

The titles of the various units within the manual weren't particularly snappy, but the book was a gold mine for the agents who were looking to build a more efficient operation. The units included: "Planning and Time Control"; "Office Facilities and Equipment"; "Office Personnel"; "Office Procedures and Forms"; "Personal Public Relations"; and "Prospecting and Sales Procedures."

Two separate but complementary manuals were also published, one called *Advanced Financial Planning Guide* and one entitled *Secretary's Manual*.

The manuals not only provided a much-needed service to the industry but also changed forever the character of the Round Table. Up to that point the Round Table had been geared to its once-a-year meeting. After each meeting copies of the speeches were printed up in what was called the *Proceedings* book, which was sent out to all members. This is not to play down the tremendous amount of year-round work that went into the planning of every Annual Meeting. But the fact remains that there were no year-round educational activities.

These first manuals provided the spark to ignite the explosive growth of the MDRT's agent education efforts. The same process characterizes all these efforts: in-depth analysis of a problem faced by an agent, followed by the finding and publishing of solutions. These efforts continue on an on-going, year-round basis.

The extensions of the original idea continue. In 1971 the Round Table published a three-part manual called *The Agent As A Businessman*. This manual dealt with accounting and financial systems for agents, forms of business organization such as sole proprietorships, partnerships and corporations within which the agent may choose to operate, and estate and financial planning for the agent. A permanent committee continues to update this manual.

In 1974 MDRT released another study entitled *How to Develop a Pension and Profit Sharing Operation*.

In 1975 *The Time Stretcher* came out of a professional study of the time management practices of 2,000 MDRT members. The results of this study were then put into practice by 20 MDRT members and their secretaries. As a result, the members of the research group saved an average of 2¼ hours per day, with an average value of $145 per hour. The time saved and/or increased money earned was utilized in many ways, including more time with family, more community activity, and more staff and equipment.

Most of these educational efforts have dealt with the individual agent's need to build a better nest. Most have also been off-shoots from or extensions of the original manuals.

It's typical of the top life insurance producers that they are constantly looking for better ways to do things. As monumental as the first study was, it was revised and updated two years later, mainly in response to suggestions by agents in the field who had put to use the systems outlined in the manuals and either proposed new ideas or developed refinements of them. Three more revisions of the manuals have been made, for the same reasons.

For example, the filing systems suggested in the original manual simply didn't work well for the average agent. So a committee of top producers worked for over three years to develop a system that was tailor-made for life insurance agents.

The new MDRT Information Retrieval System (the "Cardboard Computer"), which was introduced in 1972, is used today throughout the industry—by many life insurance companies, the major trade publications, and other trade associations.

Even today the association is exploring time-saving possibilities such as a computerized system of information retrieval that would outdate all previous systems.

This greater sophistication has also brought increased use of modern communication tools. Whereas in years past the Round Table disseminated its information only in print form, today many of the programs come in a variety of audiovisual formats so that an agent can choose the format with which he's most comfortable.

In addition to the "nest-building" educational efforts, the Round Table has explored other problem areas that have faced the agent.

For example, a 1968 study of widows showed that most agents weren't adequately trained to deal with a death claim. After an exhaustive study the Round Table published a brochure called *Humanizing The Death Claim*—the most complete guide of its kind in the business.

An interesting sidelight to the development of many of these educational programs is that the Round Table has acted as a catalyst in bringing together the life insurance companies, other trade associations, and trade publications to solve many industry-wide problems, thus helping to establish an almost continuous dialogue among the various segments that at best was sporadic in the past.

The most important fact to emerge out of all this is that these programs started becasue the individual agent in the field was faced with problems that needed a group effort to solve, and that solutions and answers were found not because institutions willed them to happen but because agents were willing to donate their time and share their ideas as part of a constant striving to better themselves and their profession.

"Build a better nest," someone said.

"We are! We will!" the agents answered.

CHAPTER ELEVEN

There's More to Life than Selling Life Insurance

In the back of everyone's head is the desire to be a whole person:

- to establish a regular pattern of exercise, diet, and weight control that will keep the body healthy (and kick those darned cigarettes, too);
- to read enlightening books and attend plays and operas that will broaden the mind;
- to devote more time to the relationship with one's spouse so that the joys of love and the intimacies known when first married can be relived;
- to get to know the children individually, on a one-to-one basis, in order to help them find their own niche;
- to set aside more time for the family so that they can work and play together as a unit;
- to be active in church or synagogue activities;
- to tackle some community problem that is worthwhile and the solution of which will have a beneficial impact on other people.

Every agent knows that there's more to life than just selling life insurance. But, being human, more often than not the agent falls into the trap of his own success. One of the traps is that the agent comes to feel that the sale of life insurance is such a great social good in itself that no other service is as important or necessary.

From his first days in the business an agent learns that the more calls made, the more sales made. With the single-minded goal of success planted up front, the agent puts on blinders and heads out for that goal. A little success breeds the desire for greater success, so, with tunnel vision, the agent continues the rapid pace. Perhaps this scenario sounds familiar:

The agent waves good-bye to his children in the morning, chats with them over dinner while his mind is churning with ideas for his evening's calls, then arrives home after the kids have gone to bed.

Saturday rolls around, and the agent's in the office, catching up on paperwork and planning for the next week. Sunday is spent reading trade literature.

And the entire time, he's patting himself on the back, not just for meeting some sales objectives or for providing so well for his family, but because by this time he's picked up considerable enthusiasm for his work and he knows what a valuable contribution he's making to the family and business lives of his clients. But what about his own life and family?

Too often, the agent wakes up when it's too late . . . maybe when he visits one of his kids in college and realizes that he's talking to a total stranger . . . or when he gets a call from a divorce lawyer.

Each individual, in his own way, eventually has to deal with his desire to be a whole person, to evaluate himself and his personal world.

The top producers in the Round Table have all wrestled with the challenges of becoming a whole person.

106

Naturally, there are always a few rare men and women who seem to accomplish everything they set out to do so easily— they're in perfect physical shape, they're involved with their kids, they have loving relationships with their spouses, they're leaders in their churches, and they make things happen when they get involved in a community project.

But these are the exceptions. Most of the top agents have had to make a considerable effort to maintain a balance in their lives.

The metamorphosis from the agent wrapped in a cocoon of work to the blossoming "whole man" usually requires some prodding. In some cases the agent gets sick, and he suddenly sees the folly of trying to work 25-hour days. Other times a spouse may be able to coax the work-obsessed agent into spending more time with the family.

Generally, however, it's the agent's peers who are able to exert the most influence on him. Sometimes the influence is direct, such as from members of his study group who, in group-therapy fashion, point out the fallacies of his ways. Sometimes the prodding comes by example, from seeing how another agent who's faced with the same problems has been able to fashion a complete life.

Members of the Round Table have from the beginning recognized the need for a life insurance underwriter to be a well-rounded person, in part for his own benefit and happiness but also to give him a better understanding of the dreams, fears, and plans of his clients—to give him a greater ability to empathize.

At first this personal side of an agent's life was mentioned only in passing at the formal meetings. The old-timers say that it was, however, often a topic of discussion during informal meetings, when the members would become more contemplative.

In the 1950s more and more emphasis was placed during the formal meetings on broadening the outlook of the agent. Several original dramas were presented that dealt with agents struggling to find their identities. Several speakers from outside the life insurance industry were also introduced during this period.

In 1961 the noted philosopher Dr. Mortimer J. Adler spoke on the subject of "The Art of Communicating" at the Annual Meeting. His talk ignited such a high level of interest in discussing subjects other than those directly related to the selling of life insurance that the Round Table invited him back in 1962 to talk about "The Parts of Life." This started a continuing program designed to develop the "whole man."

The "Whole Man Concept," as it's called, quite simply recognizes the fact that there's more to life than just selling life insurance. Each year outside speakers are invited to present ideas that will broaden the minds of the agents. The speakers over the years—many of them famous personalities—have varied widely, being drawn from the fields of philosophy, communications, religion, psychology, economics, foreign relations and trade, mental and physical fitness.

The hunger for this type of exposure to new ideas is made evident by the members' enthusiasm toward the speakers and by the ways that some of the ideas have been implemented.

Agents are the type of people who, by nature or training, try to find an application for a new idea. One year a speaker at the Annual Meeting talked in general terms about the need for a person to step back and identify his own values, then to place more emphasis on the things that he values most. The following year one of the top producers told the members that he placed such a high value on his children that he set aside one night each week to be devoted to one of them on a rotating basis.

So what started as an intangible idea was quickly translated into a reality. Many agents have since then adopted the practice and have reported the tremendous gratification this simple application of a good idea has given them.

Another speaker talked about the need for every person to set up a daily exercise program. The speaker was so effective at showing his audience the importance of starting a program immediately that many of the agents started a regular exercise schedule even before the convention ended, and hundreds have continued to the present. Many were so enthusiastic that they started comprehensive exercise programs in their communities and have influenced their clients to exercise regularly.

Another speaker, John Gardner, so impressed his audience with the need for community involvement—not just occasional fund-raising involvement, but targeting on a specific need and devoting time to a single project—that within a year over 600 members of the Round Table had located target areas and were working on them.

Although it's impossible to quantify the results of all the ideas that have been presented, it's clear that the speakers have broadened the outlook of many Round Table members.

One of the most spectacular tangible results of this broadened outlook is a book that was published in 1976 by the Round Table, called *FamilyTime: A Revolutionary Old Idea.* This book offers solutions to the deterioration of the family unit. The book is remarkable not only for what it does but also for what it reveals about the people who developed it.

First of all, the book answers a basic need. Life insurance agents, probably in equal measure to lawyers and clergy, have seen the steady breaking apart of the family as a unit. But the authors of *FamilyTime* did not produce a philosophical, negative, doomsday type of document. Rather, *FamilyTime* is a delightfully positive compilation of specific ideas for stimulating communication among family members.

Like those who developed it, *FamilyTime* does not fuss or fret about problems faced by the family. Instead, it quietly, effectively, and optimistically offers detailed ways that a person can solve the problems. Everyone who reads the book will be struck by the tenderness, the sensitivity, and the caring of those who created it.

Anyone who doubts the deep commitment of the top life insurance agents and their ability to solve complex problems should read *FamilyTime*.

The Whole Man Concept is an integral part of the educational activities of the Round Table. Because of its commitment to this concept, the Round Table will continue to present new ideas and concepts to the members in an effort to broaden their outlooks . . . to stretch their minds . . . to help them achieve a balance in their personal lives . . . to bring a higher level of awareness that will help prepare them for the many unknown challenges of the future.

CHAPTER TWELVE

Soaring into the Future

The future of the professional, skilled, and successful life insurance agent today is more secure and offers more exciting challenges and rewards than ever before in the history of the profession.

Why?

First of all, the basic selling situation is secure. Human beings are not immortal. They will continue to face death and the possibility of untimely death. The need for life insurance protection will last until someone can guarantee with certainty that a person will live to a predetermined age.

The need for agents to sell life insurance will last as long as people need to be persuaded to take action in properly protecting their loved ones and the continuation of their businesses.

Futurists talk about the coming of an impersonal society where computers will assume many day-to-day decisions, where the government will take care of all needs, where the average person will be a self-centered, uncaring, unemotional pleasure-seeker.

Some futurists even envision life insurance agents of the future as mere order-takers who will respond to a computer-

ized annual print-out of an individual's financial needs.
Hogwash!

The problem is that most futurists have never sold life insurance. If they had, they would understand the unique role the life insurance agent plays in society and how much more important this role will become in the future.

Consider the basic role of leading life insurance agents. They sell to a wide range of clientele, both individuals and businesses. They sell face-to-face, in situations that demand their involvement in the wants and needs of their clients. They must prepare life insurance plans that require them to make judgments. These judgments are often based on evaluations that the agents can't just find in rate books or sales manuals, because they include balancing the intangible dream of a client with the very tangible factor of how much the client can afford and then tempering the result with a feeling for how much the client is willing to pay. Every selling situation is different, as individualistic as a client's thumbprint, voice, or signature.

The individual tailoring that good agents do, the judgmental decisions they have to make, and the face-to-face involvements are all things that a computer will never be able to do because no one can program intangibles such as dreams and feelings.

In fact, the increasing depersonalization of society that the futurists talk about will create an atmosphere that will even increase the need for the individualized services of the life insurance agent. The good agent will represent "old" values like responsibility for others, family togetherness, individual initiative, and personal freedom, which will become increasingly treasured as big business and big government forge a faceless, numbered populace.

Agents of the future will be even more professional than they are today, better educated and better trained to deal with the increasingly complex needs of their clients. The quality of the average agent will increase as most of the incompetents and misfits that have tarnished the image of the underwriters in the past drop out of the picture.

Clients of the future will have even greater demands for the type of security life insurance buys. They'll live longer, so they'll want more protection for their retirement years. And with the onrush of technology continuing at such a breakneck pace that no one dies in the same world in which they were born, the desire for security against an increasingly uncertain future will become even more important.

Computers and modern communication tools will aid the agents of the future. Current information will be at their fingertips. Once-tedious tasks like filing and proposal writing will become so systematized that the agents will have more time in which to serve their clients more creatively.

Certainly the marketplace for life insurance will change constantly, along with changing tax laws, continued governmental regulations, the use of mass merchandizing techniques, special-interest group promotions, and other factors. But the successful agents will be able to change with the marketplace just as they have in the past, because they're so attuned to what's happening in the world around them.

Few other professions offer the diverse experiences that the selling of life insurance offers top agents, from working with every conceivable family situation—single persons, single parents, divorced individuals, traditional families—to serving the insurance needs of a wide variety of businesses. Very few people in the business world have the continuous, vivid, and kaleidoscopic personal involvement in the human condition as well as the intimate workings of business that the top agent has. In addition, leading agents are deeply involved in important civic, educational, and cultural activities that give them even greater exposure to the world around them.

With such total exposure the successful agents have a built-in radar for change. Their sensitive antennae are tuned in to the real world because they spend their lives dealing with the practical aspects of the real world. Although by nature top agents are more action-oriented than reflective, they are still quick to make adjustments in their selling to respond to different situations. The perceptive agents are acutely aware that tomorrow's world is being shaped today and that, in order to survive, their marketing practices must be shaped accordingly.

In addition, the successful agents have something going for them that will make the future seem even brighter, and that is the Million Dollar Round Table. Whereas the MDRT may seem distant to agents working on their daily schedules, it's precisely this gathering together of peers to discuss the problems and challenges of a changing marketplace that will put the most successful agents in a better position to deal with the future.

Few other professions can boast the honest interchange of ideas that is so much a part of the Round Table and its meetings. Without question, the Million Dollar Round Table of the future will continue to be a complete center of knowledge, offering educational programs dealing with nearly every phase of the agent's professional life—programs that will better prepare agents for the future.

The Annual Meeting of the Round Table will undoubtedly continue to be the fountainhead of learning, of inspiration and motivation, that it has been in the past, with an increasing awareness of the need to prepare the agents for the future even more completely.

The successful agents of today are already prepared for tomorrow. In fact, they're excited about the future. They know that in their daily lives they're tuned in to what's happening in the marketplace. They're alert to change. And most of the change they have seen has been favorable to them.

The successful agents see an increasing respect for themselves as professional financial planners. They've been seeing it for years as they have become more capable of handling more complex plans.

They've seen greater officer efficiency through the use of some of the modern computerized tools, efficiency that gives them more time to serve their clients better, more time to learn about their profession.

They've seen a greater use of life insurance to lessen the impact of inheritance taxes and to help preserve estates.

They've seen a wider use of life insurance in businesses to help assure continuity and as part of employment packages.

The successful agents know that behind them is an industry unlike any other in history. Life insurance companies guarantee what no other institution can guarantee—financial security in the future. Life insurance companies have the reserves of money that not only secure the guarantee but also bring better lives to their clients because of how the reserves are invested to stimulate free enterprise economies.

So the future for life insurance underwriters is secured not only by the solidity and integrity of the industry they represent, but also by the basic role the agents themselves occupy in society, that of professional specialists who help clients reach for the dreams of the future with a secure financial base.

Above all else they're aware that as society continues to creep toward a state of faceless numbers the consumer appreciates and needs even more the individual caring and tailor-made services offered by the professional life insurance agent.

That's the role the life insurance agents have always assumed. That will continue to be the role of the high-flying eagles of the Million Dollar Round Table as they soar into the future, optimistically accepting the challenges that come.

ACKNOWLEDGEMENTS

by Quaife M. Ward

This book is dedicated to members and leaders of the Million Dollar Round Table with whom I have shared many, many sunrises and sunsets.

These remarkable men and women and their equally remarkable organization, the Million Dollar Round Table, have imprinted my life. I have enjoyed a rare and fulfilling experience—the chance to observe an unprecedented panorama of giving and sharing and a lesson in group dynamics that I feel is without parallel in the annals of human and business relationships.

I wish to thank the present Executive Committee for making this book possible and the many Past Presidents and others who have offered encouragement and advice.

I especially appreciate the assistance received from Caleb Smith, Grant Taggart, Robert Burroughs, Ron Stever, Alfred Ostheimer III, Harold Parsons, Paul Dunnavan, Paul Cook, Theodore Widing, John Todd, Walter Hiller,* William Earls, G. Nolan Bearden, George Byrnes, Arthur Priebe,* Howard Goldman, William Davidson,* Adon Smith II, Robert Albritton, James Irvine, Jr., Lester Rosen, Alfred Lewallen,* Iram Brewster, Donald Shepherd, Frank Sullivan, Sadler Hayes, Stanley Watts,* John Ames, Richard Bowers, James Longley, Henry McCamish, Jr., C. Robinson Fish III, Jack Peckinpaugh and Rulon Rasmussen.

For their suggestions and assistance in meeting deadlines I thank Roderick Geer, Executive Vice President, and staff members John Prast, Ronald Solberg, Lawrence Bender, William Woulfe, Marjorie Davis, Rita Hammes, John Bell, Dennis Smith, Michael Ferguson, and Julia Lederer.

My special thanks to my co-author, Tedd Determan, who worked so many late hours on a tight schedule, for taking the research material I collected and condensing it down into what I feel is one of the most definitive profiles ever published of the successful life insurance agents.

Both Tedd and I are particularly indebted to Marshall Wolper and Millard Grauer for their counsel and objective criticism in their detailed review of the text. And finally a word of grateful thanks to our bright, keen-eyed, sharp-penciled editor, Laurie Braun, who polished the script so beautifully.

* Deceased

About the Authors:

QUAIFE M. WARD graduated from Iowa State University and after a number of formative years serving two large industrial corporations entered the association management field. In 1957 he was narned Executive Director of the Million Dollar Round Table and served in that capacity until 1971, when he was named Executive Consultant. He has also served as consultant to the Institute of Insurance Marketing, Louisiana State University, and to Sales Analysis Institute, Oak Brook, Illinois, a management and sales training firm.

TEDD C. DETERMAN was an Eagle Scout, a newspaper reporter for seven years (N.Y. Herald Tribune, Long Island Advance, and United Press International), a merchant seaman, and a theatrical producer. In recent years, through his company, Crocus Productions, Inc., Evanston, Illinois, he has written, directed, and produced over 500 motion pictures, filmstrips, and sales meetings, a good number of which were in the area of sales motivation. In addition, he has written speeches for the key executives of over 30 major corporations.

BIBLIOGRAPHY

This book has drawn on the following sources:

MDRT Proceedings, 1927-1976.

Annual Business Meeting Minutes and Reports, 1927-1976.

Chairmen's Summaries of Yearly Activities, 1930-1942.

Round The Table newsletters and MDRT Bulletins, 1960-1976.

The MDRT Journal, 1974-1976.

Personal Interviews and Correspondence with presidents and veteran members.

Marketing Life Insurance, J. Owen Stalson.

A Chronology of
Significant Events in MDRT
History

1927—32 Members—Paul F. Clark, CLU, Chairman—John Hancock—Peabody Hotel, Memphis, Tennessee

The first meeting of the Million Dollar Round Table was held on October 13, during the 1927 NALU Annual Meeting in the Peabody Hotel, Memphis, Tennesee. Paul Clark presided over 32 members who attended. They agreed that a permanent association be established and that George Lackey be appointed chairman with the power to select a committee to work out the details of how the new association would be structured. At the time, NALU had 15,000 members. Edward A. Woods, General Agent, Equitable-New York, was one of the few guests present. Julian Myrick, who was to first qualify for the MDRT in 1959 at age 79, was president of NALU and gave the welcoming remarks at this first meeting.

1928—38 Members—Paul Clark, CLU, Chairman—John Hancock—Book-Cadillac, Detroit, Michigan

The second meeting of the MDRT was also held during the NALU Annual Meeting in Detroit, Michigan. Paul Clark presided until George Lackey was elected chairman. William Duff discussed the need for Life membership and suggested that three successive years of qualification be established as a membership requirement.

During the business meeting it was moved by Mr. Blosser and seconded by Mr. Clegg that the MDRT of NALU be made permanent. The motion passed, and Chairman Clark moved that a committee of three be appointed to carry on the work of the MDRT. George E. Lackey was chairman of the committee, which was composed of William Duff and Earl G. Manning. After the motion was seconded and carried, it was moved and seconded that $5 be collected from each member attending the 1928 meeting to provide funds for operations. Eleanor Young Skillen (Penn Mutual), a member for one year only, was the first woman member of the MDRT.

Up to the present, William F. Duff, CLU, has been shown as being the second chairman. Someone erred. Duff was one of the original 32 members and was an interested and loyal member until his death; he was, however, never elected, nor did he serve as chairman.

1929—64 Members—George E. Lackey, CLU, Chairman—Massachusetts Mutual—Mayflower Hotel, Washington D.C.

At the third meeting of the MDRT, held in Washington D.C., George E. Lackey presided. It was established that three years of attendance at the MDRT meeting would make an agent eligible to attend for life. In order to vote or hold office an agent would have to be a Qualifying member. Annual dues of $5 were reestablished to provide members with mailing, copies of proceedings, and membership certificates. A new Nominating Committee of three was appointed to select 1930 officers.

Clay W. Hamlin's talk was hailed by members as a milestone. He emphasized the need to sell from the prospect's viewpoint, to find out his wants and needs. "Raising a $250,000 Producer to a $1,000,000 Producer" was an assigned topic discussed by a panel of eight members.

In other presentations, Theodore M. Riehle advised selling the medical exams first, then the presentation . . . and then keeping your mouth shut. On selling trust business, he opted for selling the idea, examination, life insurance, before bringing in the trust department. Another member, Clinton Davidson, a former trust officer, was the MDRT's first bona fide estate planner. He explained how to develop a sophisticated staff and deal with consultants such as lawyers, accountants.

Nathaniel Seefurth, an outstanding tax attorney, was the MDRT's first non-member speaker; the 1929 meeting was the first of many to which he was invited as a speaker.

1930—118 Members—Earl G. Manning, Chairman—John Hancock—Royal York Hotel, Toronto, Canada

At the fourth meeting of MDRT Earl G. Manning presided. The practice of using the retiring chairman on the Executive Committee for his experience and advice was established at this time. Manning led a discussion on organized publicity and sales promotion materials and advertising expenses. In addition, Manning and a trust officer in Boston organized the first meeting between agents and trust officers of banks (Junior Round Table) and held four meetings. This unofficially began the Estate Planning Councils and bank recognition programs. Attending this meeting were the first Canadian members of the MDRT, R. E. Campbell, Toronto, Canada, and Brenton S. Brown, Vancouver. H. A. Binder also delivered a presentation on advertising and promotion. MDRT's second woman member, Miss Sara Frances Jones, Chicago, attended for one year only. N. Lowndes of London and Sydney became the first overseas member. First membership certificates and buttons were issued.

1931—168 Members—Theodore M. Riehle, CLU, Chairman—Equitable-N.Y.—William Penn Hotel, Pittsburgh, Pennsylvania

At the fifth meeting of MDRT, Chairman Theodore Riehle set the tone for MDRT's quest for excellence. In his address he said, "The members of this Table are charged with the duty of being the leaders, not only for ideas, but for education, ethics and everything else that tends to raise the standards of the life insurance business."

Attending the meeting were MDRT's first Japanese members, Kinashita Shigeo, Meiji Life; Yasuyuki Oba, Meiji Life; and Nakasone Ikutara, Meiji Life all from Tokyo, Japan. Discussions about current economic conditions made members aware that businessmen were showing greater interest in life insurance and a greater appreciation for it.

For the first time, the use of life insurance in capital transfer arrangements was discussed by Earl Manning and Robert Brown. Other members discussed the increased interest in and sale of annuities.

Prior to this meeting Ted Riehle met with President Herbert Hoover to discuss insurance issues.

Other meeting highlights saw Manning P. Brown, Equitable-N.Y., Philadelphia, explain the effectiveness of using visual selling techniques. The question was raised as to why agents who sell group insurance should not be invited to be members of MDRT. Up to that time they were not invited, and the suggestion was referred to committee.

At this meeting the requirement of membership in local underwriters associations was established.

Vivian Anderson discussed the subject of professionalism and advised never to call or canvass a client without a definite interview. He also emphasized the importance of community involvement.

Jacob W. Shoul explained one of the first and most unusual "key man" sales in MDRT history when he described how he sold to his shoe manufacturing client the idea of buying insurance on the life of a large retail shoe client.

The first husband and wife members were Gertrude Brandwein, New York Life, and Samuel Brandwein, Equitable.

1932—125 Members—Robert A. Brown, Chairman—Pacific Mutual—The Fairmont, San Francisco, California

At the sixth annual meeting members discussed assigned subjects. Subjects covered by John Stevenson, H.O. Exec., included time management, selective presentations. "Prospecting" was assigned subject; 6 men talked on it. Among the assignments, Caleb Smith discussed the value of standardized sales talk (with visuals). Use of probate court records, to show estate shrinkage, as a selling tool was discussed. A. L. Abrams became the first member to discuss minimum deposit plans. The subject of gift and estate taxes was tackled by a trust officer and Vivian Anderson. Ted Kibble spoke on business insurance. General discussion at the meeting focused on annuities, life insurance as an investment, and advertising.

The first membership profile study was conducted.

1933—101 Members—M. J. Donnelly, Chairman—Equitable—N.Y.—The Stevens Hotel, Chicago, Illinois

At the seventh meeting, held in Chicago, M. J. Donnelly, Chairman, presided over 101 qualifiers, including an agent from South Africa. Donnelly continued Brown's format of assigned subjects plus an open forum.

A presentation on "The Business Outlook '33-'34" saw members discussing the merits of large numbers of cases versus large policies. At the time, employers were dropping their group insurance and replacing it with salary savings plans. Agents discussed annuities and insuring juveniles and women as an alternative way to replace business they were losing. Paul Clark urged members to observe and retain original objectives of MDRT: to produce $1 million in volume and to maintain the association's exclusivity and confidentiality. Other subjects included business operations, life insurance trusts, advertising and promotion, and business insurance.

Fred Goldstandt described how he was forced to turn to the annuity business. During the Depression, underwriting rules were tightened substantially and insurance companies would not accept policies as large as in 1929.

Members voiced concern about the underwriting policies of companies that discouraged large producers by placing severe limitations on an individual's maximum coverage—thus making it difficult to write large amounts of insurance. One member said the MDRT should speak out and take action.

Decades ahead of many in the field, Tom Scott spoke on the subject of time conservation and said that many MDRT members do not requalify because they are spending more time on service than sales. He urged members to save time by using the mail, telephone, and staff. Also ahead of his time was Harry Wright, who was closing two-thirds of his cases in his own office merely by asking clients to meet with him there!

1934—118 Members—Thomas M. Scott, Chairman—Penn Mutual—The Schroeder Hotel, Milwaukee, Wisconsin

At the eighth meeting, held in Milwaukee, Thomas M. Scott, Chairman, presided. Harry T. Wright, in a presentation entitled "The MDRT Producer's Problem," stressed the role of proper mental attitude. "The only thing that we are paid for," he said, "is seeing people in relation to new business."

Other subjects included Caleb Smith on servicing old policyholders; F. Jean Little on family income policies; Stuart Smith on key man business insurance; Lou Behr on prospecting; and Wallace King on organization and delegation.

At this meeting Earl Manning displayed one of the earliest consumer guides on the subject of purchasing life insurance. Entitled "Economic Life Insurance Purchase Guide," it contained a message that still rings true today: agents should "talk about what policies will do, rather than what they are."

Another noteworthy highlight was the attendance of Mariano R. Pesquera from San Juan, Puerto Rico, the first MDRT member from a U. S. possession.

1935—124 Members—Caleb R. Smith, Chairman, Massachusetts Mutual —The Savery Hotel, Des Moines, Iowa

At the ninth meeting Caleb Smith, Chairman, concentrated on three main topics: (1) life insurance for tax purposes; (2) business insurance; and (3) annuities and their uses.

Speakers included Dr. Albright on key man insurance; Julius Eisendrath on partnership and sole proprietorship insurance ("Would you like to be in business with your partner's wife?"); Paul Clark on gift and inheritance taxes; Eugene Stinde on business insurance; John Morrell and Stuart Smith on annuities.

A revised insignia of the MDRT was introduced at this meeting.

1936—143 Members—Harry T. Wright, Chairman, Equitable-N.Y.—Ritz Carlton Hotel, Boston, Massachusetts

At the tenth meeting Harry T. Wright, Chairman, presided. Wright was strict on applicants for membership and established the use of standard MDRT application forms. In addition, for the first time applicants had to furnish letters, certifying to their production, signed by their general agents or managers. Wright also for the first time established the practice of verifying memberships of applicants in their local underwriters associations.

The first pre-meeting outing of members was held. Several future chairmen attended their first meeting—Robert Burroughs, H. Kennedy Nickell, Ron Stever, Alfred Ostheimer III, and John O. Todd. These five also formed the nucleus of what is believed to be the first voluntary study group of MDRT members. By September Grant Taggart, who started in the business in 1918, had sold 4,000 policies, averaging well over 200 per year, with nearly $14,000,000 in force.

1937—158 Members—Grant Taggart, Chairman, California-Western States Life—Brown Palace Hotel, Denver, Colorado

The eleventh meeting of the MDRT was presided over by Grant Taggart.

In 1936 MDRT members averaged 85 cases with an average policy of $15,000 and a volume of $1,300,000. This year's program featured a great expansion of speakers and topics: Louis Behr on prospecting; Ron Stever on prospecting and use of phone; Hyman Rogal on community goodwill; Phinnias Prouty on prospecting via lawyers and investment counselors; Julian Schwab on time control.

By 1936 the MDRT had influenced $63,625,000 worth of business to trust companies.

George Lackey spoke on cooperation with attorneys.

Other speakers were Eugene Stinde and Paul Sanborn on business insurance; Paul Cook on majority versus minority stock interests; Edward J. Dore, Burt Wulfekoetter, and Nathaniel Seefurth on taxation.

1938—162 Members—Jack Lauer, Chairman—The Rice Hotel, Houston, Texas

The twelfth MDRT meeting featured the first appearance of Denis Maduro, who later became legal counsel for the MDRT. At the meeting the first official MDRT Bylaws were adopted by a vote of 24 to 6. In addition, a $200,000 limit on group credits was established, as well as a 50 percent limit on group and single premium and annual premium annuity credits.

Other highlights of the year included two profile surveys of members, dues were increased from $5 to $10 per year, and the first company certifying letters were required.

1939—163 Members—Paul C. Sanborn, Chairman—Connecticut Mutual —Jefferson Hotel, St. Louis, Missouri

The 13th Annual Meeting featured Elliott Roosevelt as speaker. Mrs. Anna S. Richardson, director of Crowell-Collier Publishing Co., spoke on "The Consumer's Viewpoint."

A special meeting was held this year in New York City. At the meeting Denis Maduro presented a special paper on pensions. The paper was later printed and sold for $3 per copy.

1940—154 Members—Henry G. Mosler, Chairman—Massachusetts Mutual. —Bellevue Stratford, Philadelphia, Pennsylvania

The Annual Meeting program dealt with emphasis on prospecting, sales approach, and the presentation. Also discussed at the 14th Annual Meeting was the capital transfer idea.

A Bylaws revision was passed, making the qualifying period for the 1941 Round Table any 12 consecutive months from January 1, 1940, to July 1, 1941.

1941—171 Members—H. Kennedy Nickell, CLU, Chairman—Connecticut General—Netherlands Plaza, Cincinnati, Ohio

The MDRT climbed out of the membership slump caused by the Depression. Total membership of 171 in 1941 surpassed the 1931 membership of 168.

A minimum requirement of 10 lives or cases was approved at this meeting as a Bylaws requirement. This was the 15th year of the MDRT and four of the original 32 members were present for a reunion. The four were Darby, Donnelly, Lackey, and Spencer.

1942—233 Members—Robert P. Burroughs, Chairman—National Life-Vermont—No meeting was held because of World War II

Members voted by mail not to have the meeting. However, a special paper, prepared by Denis Maduro, was mailed to all members.

Al Ostheimer and Ron Stever published in book form papers on sales ideas from various members. This was sent to the members along with a membership directory and an extensive profile study of all MDRT members. This was the last year the Round Table was governed by a three-man Executive Committee.

1943—232 Members—Ron Stever, CLU, Chairman—Equitable—N.Y.—William Penn, Pittsburgh, Pennsylvania

In 1943 the five-man Executive Committee was approved and became operative. The revised Bylaws, as adopted on September 13, 1943, were also approved and went into effect. Also in 1943 the Executive Committee recorded the minutes of its meetings for the first time.

1944—408 Members—Alfred J. Ostheimer III, Chairman—Northwestern Mutual—The Statler, Detroit, Michigan

For the first time the Executive Committee approved reimbursement of the chairman's secretarial expenses up to $500. It was also the first year that the company of the chairman sponsored and paid for a dinner for all members at the Annual Meeting.

A proposal for local MDRT chapters was also discussed. It was agreed that members should be able to meet and exchange ideas but that they could not use MDRT's name. A bylaw was drafted accordingly.

At this meeting insignia rules were also revised. The insignia was redesigned and the first insignia rule book was published. There was some conflict with NALU relating to the scheduling of the MDRT Annual Meeting during the NALU Annual Meeting.

A total of 20 ammendments to the Bylaws were proposed and passed in this year. Members felt that programming at the Annual Meeting in the years prior to 1944 had overemphasized pensions, and asked that a better balance be sought.

Up to 1944 nearly 40 percent of the members had been Life only members. The Executive Committee felt that a greater majority of members should be in the Qualifying & Life and Qualifying classifications, so a successful drive was initiated in 1944.

The 1944 application forms became the prototypes for the future in terms of format, instructions, the notarized affidavit of membership in a local association, the certifying letter format, etc. Al Ostheimer also designed a checklist form for each application to facilitate processing. He also used the "holler" form letter designed by Ron Stever to simplify correspondence with applicants.

1945—468 Members—John E. Clayton, Chairman—Massachusetts Mutual —no Annual Meeting because of World War II

Lou Behr was assigned the task of publishing and distributing a book on sales ideas in lieu of the meeting. Massachusetts Mutual provided the funds to bind the book with a hard cover with each member's name printed on his copy.

1946—525 Members—Louis Behr, CLU, Chairman—Equitable Life-New York—French Lick Springs Hotel, French Lick, Indiana

Lou Behr, the chairman, became ill and could neither preside over nor attend his Annual Meeting. He did not recover from his illness and died while still in office.

This was the first year that the MDRT held its meeting in a location physically removed from the NALU Annual Meeting.

Membership dues were still $10. However, because of increased expenses, a special assessment (the MDRT's first and only one) of $7.50 was voted and approved by the membership. At this meeting the Bylaws Committee was made a standing committee.

In 1946 there were only three agents on NALU's 16-man Board of Trustees.

Because the 1946 meeting was the 20th anniversary of the MDRT, it included a considerable amount of information on the beginnings of the Million Dollar Round Table.

1947—726 Members—Harold S. Parsons, Chairman—Travelers—New Ocean House, Swampscott, Massachusetts

Applications for membership were sent out in January, 1947, with a deadline of June 30. Membership breakdown was 374 Qualifying, 245 Qualifying & Life, and 107 Life—a healthy balance.

Company rank was: Northwestern, 131; Massachusetts Mutual, 55; Nel York Life, 52; Equitable, 43; New England, 37; Mutual Benefit, 33; Penn Mutual, 30; John Hancock, 22; and MONY, 20.

1948—829 Members—Paul H. Dunnavan, CLU, Chairman—Canada Life —French Lick Springs, French Lick, Indiana

This year marked a dramatic change in handling speakers' manuscripts. Prior to 1948 speakers had to submit a manuscript prior to the meeting so that it could be reproduced and handed out to registrants and press. For the 1948 meeting speakers did not have to submit their manuscripts.

Dunnavan sent out a sophisticated membership profile questionnaire. He also wrote an extensive memo on the handling of MDRT correspondence and work. Dues were increased from $10 to $17.50.

Dunnavan had four concurrent bull sessions one evening at the 1948 Annual Meeting. These covered: (1) personal organization and management; (2) personal insurance, simple programming, and estate planning; (3) pension and profit sharing and deferred compensation; and (4) business insurance. This was an innovation in programming.

Dunnavan also had as a guest speaker an outstanding industrial psychologist, Dr. Perry L. Rohrer. Dr. Rohrer was associated with Rohrer, Hibler, and Replogy.

1949—824 Members—Paul W. Cook, CLU, Chairman—Mutual Benefit —Netherlands Plaza, Cincinnati, Ohio

Fortune magazine did a feature article on the MDRT in 1949. Paul Cook reversed Dunnavan's policy and required manuscripts from all speakers pior to the meeting for distribution to registrants.

Harriet Preinetz, the first paid employee of the MDRT, was hired and was located in the first permanent headquarters office at 1 N. LaSalle St., Chicago, Illinois.

1950—790 Members—Theodore Widing, CLU, Chairman—Provident Mutual—Haddon Hall, Atlantic City, New Jersey

The National Quality Award was promoted. Fifty-five percent of the 1948 Round Table had received the NQA. Three reprints of Annual Meeting speeches were offered for sale to members to send to clients.

At the Annual Meeting there was a display of MDRT members' prestige mailings to clients and prospects, sales ideas, and testimonials. This was a first and was well-received. The first new man reception was planned with Paul Cook as chairman. Each new man received a special printed invitation.

Dues in 1950 were $25. The Annual Meeting registration fee was $20.

1951—949 Members—John O. Todd, CLU, Chairman—Northwestern Mutual—Coronado Hotel, Coronado, California

The first room-hopping sessions took place. This meeting also featured the first reception for speakers and committee members and the first dramatic presentation, "The Education of Richard Rowe."

Chairman Todd, in a letter to the Executive Committee, raised a question about the function and objectives of the MDRT. He asked, "Should it (MDRT) engage in worthwhile projects which would benefit the industry?" The response was negative. It was felt that the MDRT should continue sticking to its basic objectives.

The practice of the chairman's company sponsoring a dinner at the Annual Meeting was discontinued this year. In lieu of the dinner, the company provided a favor for each registrant.

The MDRT letterhead, which listed all chairmen from 1927-1950, was redesigned in this year. California-Western States, Occidental, and Pacific Mutual sponsored the banquet at the Annual Meeting.

1952—1,065 Members—Walter N. Hiller, CLU, Chairman—Penn Mutual—Fort Washington Hotel, Bretton Woods, New Hampshire

The play *Stardust*, written by Laflin Jones of Northwestern Mutual Life for the MDRT, was produced and presented at the Annual Meeting. This was the 25th anniversary of the Round Table, and an anniversary dinner was held.

Bylaws changes made in 1952 included the definition of Round Table membership as a privilege rather than a right. The Bylaws changes also refined the Executive Committee's responsibilities in granting and denying membership in the MDRT.

1953—1,240 Members—William T. Earls, CLU, Chairman—Mutual Benefit Life—The Greenbrier, White Sulphur Springs, West Virginia

The Greenbrier-MDRT Profile brochure about the MDRT and its members was produced as a prestige piece for use by members with clients. Printed Annual Meeting committee reports were prepared for the first time.

George Byrnes was program chairman, and he developed detailed and explicit instructions to his committee chairmen. These letters became prototypes for the future.

The Executive Committee authorized the chairman to engage public relations counsel to handle publicity for the Annual Meeting (a first) and for the members who attended.

Attendance at the 1953 Annual Meeting was 557, an astounding 45 percent of the membership.

There were eight women qualifiers in 1953. Up to then, 29 women had qualified for the Round Table. In 1953, 26 percent of the membership were CLUs.

Of the 32 original members in 1927, five were still members. These five were Paul Clark, R. V. Darby, M. J. Donnelly, L. A. Spencer, and Sam Weems.

Of the 39 who attended the 1928 meeting, 14 were still members. These 14 were Paul Clark, R. V. Darby, M. J. Donnelly, L. A. Spencer, Sam Weems, Julius M. Eisendrath, Gerald Eubank, H. G. Feldman, Clay W. Hamlin, Jack Lauer, Thomas M. Scott, Lawrence E. Simon, Stuart F. Smith, and Dix Teachenor.

It was also at this time that detailed written critiques of the Annual Meeting were requested. These were submitted to the next program chairman for use in planning the next meeting.

1954—1,492 Members—G. Nolan Bearden, Chairman—New England Life —Hotel del Coronado, Coronado, California

Codification of committee functions continued. Walter N. Hiller was named membership secretary and as such assumed the responsibility of working with the MDRT staff and Executive Committee in reviewing and approving membership applications.

A second full-time staff person was hired. Harriet Preinitz was given the title of executive secretary. A consultant was retained to help present a case study at the Annual Meeting.

The Executive Committee began to show concern about the companies subsidizing the expenses of their agents attending the MDRT meeting.

1955—1,557 Members—George W. Byrnes, CLU, Chairman—New England Life—The Greenbrier, White Sulphur Springs, West Virginia

This is the first year in which written reports of all committee activities were required.

This was also the first year a Public Relations Committee was appointed.

131

Dave Marks was chairman. One of its significant recommendations was for the MDRT to consider establishing a tax-exempt charitable and educational foundation supported by the members.

The first Canadian session was scheduled at the Annual Meeting. In this year, too, the MDRT was invited to move to Washington, D.C., and locate its headquarters in space provided in the new NALU building.

The possibility of hiring an Executive Director for the Round Table was discussed for the first time. It was also the first year that program notes were published for the Annual Meeting.

New man orientation procedures were being refined by James Irvine. Considerable study was made for a volume-premium-commission requirement for qualification, but nothing came of it.

The MDRT dues were $25, and the Annual Meeting registration fee was $40.

1956—2,013 Members—Arthur F. Priebe, CLU, Chairman—Penn Mutual —Meeting on the Kungsholm to Bermuda

This was the first meeting held aboard ship. Dues were $40. The Executive Committee went to the companies to determine to what extent which companies were subsidizing the expenses of their agents at the MDRT Annual Meeting. The Executive Committee asked the companies to cease paying such subsidies.

Priebe requested that Penn Mutual, his company, make a monetary gift to the MDRT instead of giving a gift to each MDRT member.

The Executive Committee also became concerned about the use of names similar to MDRT for some companies' production clubs. Consideration was given to copyrighting the MDRT name.

The Executive Committee began to consider paying office and secretarial expenses of Executive Committee members other than the chairman. Consideration was also given to the possibility of incorporating the MDRT, but nothing came of it. Hiller continued to serve as membership secretary.

1957—2,438 Members—Howard D. Goldman, CLU, Chairman—Northwestern Mutual—The Greenbrier, White Sulphur Springs, West Virginia

Q. M. Ward was hired as the first Executive Director of the Million Dollar Round Table in 1957. In that year the MDRT also filed for and received tax exemption as a 501 C6 voluntary business association.

MDRT for the first time provided scholarships to the Purdue and Southern Methodist Institutes of Insurance Marketing. Two concurrent MDRT profile studies were initiated, one by Dr. Robert Khan of the University of Michigan's Research Center and the other by Francis Merritt. Also in 1957 an MDRT staff retirement plan was begun.

The National Quality Award was discussed again as an MDRT membership requirement, as was a probationary period for applicants, but both ideas were shelved.

1958—2,987 Members—William D. Davidson, CLU, Chairman—Equitable —N.Y.—Hotel Banff, Banff, Canada

Significant Bylaws changes were adopted in 1958. These included the establishment of 21 years as a minimum age requirement for membership and a tightened requirement of six consecutive years or 10 aggregate years of qualifying membership for Life membership.

The $250,000 limit for term credit was eliminated, level term was credited at 25 percent, and decreasing term was credited at 12½ percent of face or commuted value as a result of the Bylaws changes. No credit was allowed for creditors' group insurance, a limit of $25,000 credit for insurance on an agent's own life was established, and the MDRT seriously considered adopting the National Quality Award as a membership requirement.

In 1958 The Round Table began a campaign to get companies to change the names of their production clubs where the name included MDRT terminology. A Bylaw which would require companies to meet certain qualifications was considered, and legal steps to copyright the MDRT name and insignia were initiated.

In this year a standard format for the description of each committee was implemented. The description included the composition, function, procedures, and responsibility of each committee.

1959—2,688 Members—Adon N. Smith II, CLU, Chairman—Northwestern Mutual—Americana Hotel, Bal Harbour, Florida

The membership figures decreased in 1959 as a result of the more stringent requirements adopted in 1958. Also in 1959 the MDRT Foundation was organized and established.

At the 1959 Annual Meeting the presidents of the American Bar Association, Trust Division, American Bankers Association, and the American Institute of Certified Public Accountants were invited as guests. Of the 1959 Round Table membership, 65 percent received the National Quality Award.

1960—3,040 Members—Robert S. Albritton, CLU, Chairman—Provident Mutual—Hawaiian Village Hotel, Honolulu, Hawaii

A tidal wave hit Hawaii during the Annual Meeting. Luckily no one was hurt or lost. Members had been allowed to bring their wives and families.

Round the Table began publication in this year, in the form of a newsletter. MDRT member James B. Longley, CLU completed the first index of subjects and authors in all Proceedings back to 1954.

The Story of the Round Table, a brochure, was produced and made available to members to send to clients with announcement cards. Insignia and advertising rules were revised and published, and Annual Meeting postcards were also produced and sold.

In 1960 a number of MDRT members, including Kenneth V. Robinson, William McCoy, J. Welldon Currie, Ed Wood, Ed Mintz, and Art Priebe, traveled around the world meeting insurance company officials and agents. These contacts stimulated great interest in the Round Table and had a direct effect on the increase in membership from other countries.

For the first time the MDRT and NALU Executive Committees held a joint breakfast meeting during NALU's convention.

1961—2,932 Members—James B. Irvine Jr., CLU, Chairman—National Life-Vermont—Americana Hotel, Bal Harbour, Florida

In 1961 the MDRT initiated a bank recognition program, the forerunner of today's Financial Institutions Program. The Round Table also discussed the idea of a probationary period for membership, considered changing the chairman's title to president, and talked about the idea of a company qualification requirement.

An MDRT Foundation grant of $5,000 was awarded to the American Association of University Teachers of Insurance for the development of a casebook on insurance, and the South Africa Life Underwriters Association was organized under the leadership of MDRT member Samuel "Chummy" Hirschmann.

Dr. Mortimer J. Adler was a featured speaker at the Annual Meeting; his talk, "The Art of Communicating," launched what has come to be MDRT's Whole Man Concept.

1962—3,122 Members—Lester A. Rosen, CLU, Chairman—Union Central—Queen Elizabeth Hotel, Montreal, Canada

A bylaws amendment establishing the Provisional Applicant status was passed, the company qualification requirement was revoked, the bank recognition programs were expanded, and the campaign to continue to eliminate "million clubs" was continued.

Members were srurveyed in this year to find out the number of trusts and wills they generated. MDRT member Ippei Hara took initial steps toward organizing the Japan Life Underwriters Association. Dues were set at $50 and a filing fee was established for the first time.

Paul Emile Cardinal Leger helped launch the Annual Meeting. He gave the Whole Man Concept a boost, as did Dr. Mortimer J. Adler, who returned to talk about "The Parts of Life."

1963—3,240 Members—Daniel H. Coakley, Chairman—New York Life —Meeting on the Kungsholm to Bermuda

In 1963 the Million Dollar Round Table made the Provisional Applicant status official, beginning with the 1964 Table. Also in this year the first bank recognition program kit was designed and produced.

The Executive Committee retained Howard Sigmund as public relations counsel.

MDRT also initiated discussion about a book on the Round Table, as well as the possibility of an MDRT tax letter. Work continued throughout the year on the decision to end company expense subsidies to members attending MDRT's Annual Meetings.

A member, Frank Manning, suggested that a special Round Table of Qualifying and Life members within the Table be organized.

1964—3,202 Members—Alfred J. Lewallen, CLU, President—Mutual Benefit Life—Diplomat Hotel, Hollywood, Florida

The chairman's title was changed to president. Lewallen was the only one to serve as both. The first long-range planning committee was appointed.

The MDRT Office Efficiency Manual Committee was formed in 1964, with Marshall I. Wolper, CLU, as chairman. The Advanced Financial Planning Guide Committee was formed with C. Robinson Fish III, CLU as chairman, and the *Secretary's Manual*, by Millard J. Grauer, CLU, was printed and made available to members.

The Executive Committee met in Lucerne, Switzerland, to inspect the site as a possible Annual Meeting location. Fairbanks Associates was engaged to do a management study for the MDRT; talks between MDRT, AALU, and NALU about a marriage between AALU and NALU continued.

Daniel Coakley died while serving as Immediate Past President on the Executive Committee.

1965—3,636 Members—Iram H. Brewster, President—Phoenix Mutual —the Broadmoor, Colorado Springs, Colorado

The *Personal and Office Efficiency Manual* was published and introduced at the Annual Meeting by Marshall I. Wolper, CLU. The *Advanced Financial Planning Guide*, by C. Robinson Fish III, CLU was also published and introduced. The MDRT brochure *Invitation to Excellence* was written and published for use by members and companies.

In a joint venture with the American Institute of Certified Public Accountants, a standard information form was designed to be used by accounting firms to obtain policy information from insurance companies. Frank E. Sullivan, CLU, chaired the committee working on this project. He also designed the new MDRT converter form for determining MDRT volume credits, which was approved.

A group hospital and accident plan for staff was approved in this year, as was key man insurance on the Executive Director. Recommendations by Fairbanks Associates based on its management study were accepted and implemented. The Association of Life Underwriters of Mexico asked to be accredited in 1965; the MDRT Foundation gave ten $1,000 scholarships to different colleges and universities. It also funded a widow's study by Dr. Franklin Evans. A plaque commemorating the founding of the MDRT was mounted in the Peabody Hotel, the site of the first Annual Meeting.

Article II, Purposes of the MDRT *Constitution and Bylaws* was revised and approved by the members.

1966—4,076 Members—Donald Shepherd, President—John Hancock— Statler Hilton Hotel—Boston, Massachusetts

The decision to revise the entire *Constitution and Bylaws* was made. Perrin Stryker was retained to write *The Incomparable Salesmen*.

The decision to separate MDRT's annual report from the Annual Meeting *Proceedings* was made; a tax letter, the *Newscast*, was initiated as a service to members

Harriet Preinitz, MDRT's first employee, resigned January 31, 1966. An executive health bulletin was offered to members; the joint MDRT-NALU Executive Committee breakfast was discontinued by mutual agreement; the MDRT Foundation received its 501 C3 tax exemption. Dues were $75.

1967—4,616 Members—Frank E. Sullivan, CLU, President—American United Life—Congress Hall, Lucerne, Switzerland

The *Information Manual* was developed and published in 1967, and a major revision of the *Manual on Personal and Office Efficiency* was begun. *The Incomparable Salesmen*, by Perrin Stryker, was completed and published.

MDRT again began consideration of a persistency requirement. The use of the National Quality Award as a requirement also came up. Consideration was given to hiring a technical consultant to help stage the Annual Meeting. The legal firm of Jenner and Block was approved as legal counsel for the Round Table.

The MDRT Foundation started thinking of funding the MDRT Foundation Hall on the American College campus in Bryn Mawr, Pennsylvania.

1968—5,078 Members—Sadler Hayes, President—Penn Mutual—Masonic Auditorium, San Francisco, California

Recodification of MDRT's Bylaws was completed in 1968. A policy manual and management guide for the Executive Committee were approved, and the decision to incorporate the MDRT was made.

Also in 1968 TelePrompter Corporation was retained to help stage the Annual Meeting, the Committee for Individual Involvement was appointed, and consideration of changing the fiscal year and term of office of officers from November 1—October 31 to September 1—August 31 began.

1969—5,689 Members—Stanley S. Watts, CLU, President—Equitable — N.Y.—Diplomat Hotel, Hollywood, Florida

Bylaw changes requiring the CLU designation for first-time Qualifying and Life membership and a persistency requirement were passed. Credit for disability income insurance was considered.

The amendment to the Bylaws allowing the president and Executive Committee to take office September 1 was passed, and an amendment deleting all references to NALU in MDRT's name was considered.

MDRT's tax letter, the "Newscast," was discontinued. TelePrompter Corporation was again retained to help stage the Annual Meeting. The search for a new headquarters location was begun.

This was the first year in which all Annual Meeting sessions were taped and offered for sale. The Educational Services Committee was established, the Membership Committee was given full authority in handling membership cases except revocation, termination, or suspension; and the Foundation project to fund the Foundation Hall at American College of Life Underwriters was approved.

1970—6,675 Members—John H. Ames, CLU, President—Mutual Benefit Life—Hawaiian Village, Honolulu, Hawaii

MDRT initiated discussions with the American College of Life Underwriters regarding a joint venture videotaping program, the Executive Committee authorized the hiring of an assistant executive director, and MDRT staff was restructured. The president also inaugurated the policy of sending personal letters to all new Honor Roll members.

"Certified Applicant" status was changed to "Provisional Applicant." First family night at an MDRT Annual Meeting was programmed as "Sounds of Hawaii." And the first special session ever for spouses was in the program.

The policy of the MDRT staff serving the MDRT Foundation was terminated and the Foundation began developing its own staff.

1971—7,589 Members—Richard G. Bowers, CLU, President—New York Life—Washington Hilton, Washington, D.C.

The new Budget and Finance, Speakers Bureau, and Public Industry Relations Committees and the Membership Relations Task Force were appointed. The Long Range Planning Committee was reappointed and the Committee for Individual Involvement was phased out to become a part of NALU's Public Service Program.

A management study by Lester B. Knight and Associates was initiated, all company subsidies to Executive Committee members while serving on the Executive Committee were discontinued, as were gifts to members at the Annual Meeting. The Executive Committee expense reimbursement policy was also revised in this year.

Roderick L. Geer was hired as Executive Director to replace Q. M. Ward who became Executive Consultant in 1971. The entire staff was reorganized into basic departments—Publishing, Public Relations, Administration, Educational Services, Programs and Meetings, Personnel, and Executive—with functions defined. Correspondence guidelines for the Executive Committee, staff and committees were established.

138

1972—8,361 Members—James B. Longley, CLU, President—New England Life—Queen Elizabeth Hotel, Montreal, Canada

The MDRT Foundation Hall was dedicated at the American College of Life Underwriters in Bryn Mawr, Pennsylvania. The *Information Retrieval System* was completed, published, and presented to the members. The persistency requirement was approved.

The Human Resources Valuation Committee was appointed and the worldwide Membership Relations Committee network evolved. The MDRT decided to sponsor an industry forum, and there was a special meeting between the Executive Committee and three company presidents.

Henry F. McCamish, CLU, initiated the idea of an MDRT-sponsored policyholder service study; MDRT's official name became Million Dollar Round Table, dropping the phrase "of the National Association of Life Underwriters." The MDRT trademark was registered in all major countries.

1973—9,587 Members—Henry F. McCamish, Jr., CLU, President—Massachusetts Mutual—Seattle Center, Seattle, Washington

The Human Resources Valuation Committee was appointed, and codification of Executive Committee decisions and bylaws interpretations was completed. The Ad Hoc Committee to study the organizational and management mechanism of the Round Table was appointed, and the 1972 Membership Profile Study was published.

MDRT began the policy of inviting a greater number of life insurance company executive officers to the Annual Meeting, the *Annual Meeting in Review* was written by staff, the first joint meeting of all committee chairmen and task force chairmen took place, and the first issue of *Round the Table Quarterly* was published. It also marked the first year of the Annual Meeting *Daily News*.

1974—10,987 Members—C. Robinson Fish III CLU, President—Northwestern Mutual Life—Fontainbleau Hotel, Miami Beach, Florida

MDRT headquarters moved from downtown Chicago to suburban Des Plaines in October. The Manpower Selection Committee was formed and, subsequently, Hay Associates was retained to work out a performance rating system for committee chairmen and members.

The Agent/Staff Development Committee was appointed and held its first meeting; the new manual, *How to Develop A Pension and Profit Sharing Operation*, was published. An Information Retrieval index for agency management was produced and the MDRT Blue Ribbon Committee for Advanced Achievement was appointed.

The first *Cost of Doing Business Survey* of MDRT members was initiated by the Agent As A Businessman task force; a private firm conducted an audit of the Round Table's public relations activities. The *Advanced Financial Planning Guide* was phased out after ten years of existence, and Buyers Laboratory, Inc., an advisory service, was established to help members with the purchase of office equipment.

The 50th Anniversary Committee with John Ames, CLU, Chairman, was appointed.

1975—12,422 Members—Jack Peckinpaugh, CLU, President—Indianapolis Life—Masonic Auditorium, San Francisco, California

The appointment of six divisional vice presidents to oversee assigned committee operations and to serve with the Executive Committee on the Management Council was announced. The MDRT Foundation made two grants of $25,000 each to the Widow's Consultation Center, New York City, and the National Office for Social Responsibility.

Work on the *FamilyTime* program was begun, and the report *Services to the Life Insurance Policyowner/Consumer* by the Center for Insurance Research, Georgia State University, was released. The study was underwritten by the Round Table.

The Research Committee and the Marketing Committee were appointed; videotapes of Annual Meeting sessions were offered for sale for the first time. Slide presentations used at the Annual Meeting were also made available for purchase for the first time.

In January, 1975, James B. Longley, CLU, president of the MDRT in 1972, was inaugurated governor of Maine.

1976—11,804 Members—Rulon E. Rasmussen, CLU, President—New York Life—Hynes Auditorium, Boston, Massachusetts

FamilyTime: A Revolutionary Old Idea was introduced to the public via a press conference at the Annual Meeting in Boston. The persistency requirement, the production requirement of $1.25 million, and the requirement of a CLU designation for first-time Qualifying and Life members became effective this year.

The Eden Method, Philip Eden's book on estimating the value of human life, was made available; the *Time Stretcher* was completed and made available for purchase; and the Agent/Staff Development Series was completed and published.

Late in the year the membership passed a two-year moratorium on the persistency requirement so as to allow time to work out administrative problems relating to it; the MDRT Speakers Bureau held its first Estate Planning Seminar.

A "Special Achievement" session for MDRT high-volume producers was held. The same committee subsequently established the "Top of the Table," a subgroup of the Round Table consisting initially of members who produce a minimum of $5 million in new business in a single year.